200 easy mexican recipes

D1509671

641.5972 Cof

Coffeen, K.
200 easy Mexican recipes.

PRICE: $22.88 (3710/an/la)

INNISFIL PUBLIC LIBRARY
P.O. BOX 7049
INNISFIL, ON L9S 1A8

200 easy
mexican
recipes

Authentic recipes
from burritos to enchiladas

Kelley Cleary Coffeen

Robert
ROSE

200 Easy Mexican Recipes
Text copyright © 2013 Kelley Cleary Coffeen
Recipe photographs copyright © 2013 Robert Rose Inc.
Other photographs copyright © 2013 iStockphoto.com (see details below)
Cover and text design copyright © 2013 Robert Rose Inc.

No part of this publication may be reproduced, stored in a retrieval system or transmitted, in any
form or by any means, without the prior written consent of the publisher or a license from the
Canadian Copyright Licensing Agency (Access Copyright). For an Access Copyright license, visit
www.accesscopyright.ca or call toll-free: 1-800-893-5777.

For complete cataloguing information, see page 213.

Disclaimer

The recipes in this book have been carefully tested by our kitchen and our tasters. To the best of
our knowledge, they are safe and nutritious for ordinary use and users. For those people with food
or other allergies, or who have special food requirements or health issues, please read the suggested
contents of each recipe carefully and determine whether or not they may create a problem for you.
All recipes are used at the risk of the consumer.

We cannot be responsible for any hazards, loss or damage that may occur as a result of any recipe use.

For those with special needs, allergies, requirements or health problems, in the event of any doubt,
please contact your medical adviser prior to the use of any recipe.

Design and production: Daniella Zanchetta/PageWave Graphics Inc.
Editor: Carol Sherman
Copy Editor: Karen Campbell-Sheviak
Food Photographer: Colin Erricson
Associate Food Photographer: Matt Johannsson
Food Stylist: Kathryn Robertson
Prop Stylist: Charlene Erricson

Other photographs: GROUP 1: Fajitas al sombrero © iStockphoto.com/Debbi Smirnoff; Agave ©
iStockphoto.com/Melissa Englert; Adivino-Pyramid at Uxmal © iStockphoto.com/Jan-Dirk Hansen;
Cinco de Mayo dancer © iStockphoto.com/Lorena Altamirano; Stack of tostadas © iStockphoto.com/
Juanmonino; Mexican paper flowers © iStockphoto.com/Lauri Wiberg; Tomatillo salsa verde ©
iStockphoto.com/Toru Uchida; GROUP 2: Crushing red chile peppers © iStockphoto.com/Gordana
Jovanovic; Salsa fresca © iStockphoto.com/Raul Taborda; Organic avocados at market © iStockphoto.
com/Kathrin Axer; Cactus and vintage door © iStockphoto.com/Teck Siong Ong; Let's dance! (skirt
detail) © iStockphoto.com/Terrance Emerson; Margarita © iStockphoto.com/Danny Hooks; Agave
© iStockphoto.com/Roberto A Sanchez; Sombreros © iStockphoto.com/Robert Simon; GROUP 3:
Mariachi © iStockphoto.com/Cristian Lazzari; Mexican ceramic plates © iStockphoto.com/YinYang;
Guacamole © iStockphoto.com/CactuSoup; Mayan hieroglyphs (detail) © iStockphoto.com/
Somatuscani; Tacos © iStockphoto.com/Arturo Peña Romano Medina; Red posole © iStockphoto.com/
jmalov; Bundled peppers © iStockphoto.com/Mark Jensen; GROUP 4: Making guacamole ©
iStockphoto.com/Lew Robertson; San Miguel de Allende © iStockphoto.com/Bryan Busovicki;
Organic key limes © iStockphoto.com/jmalov; Tequila shot © iStockphoto.com/Jiri Hera; Making
gorditas © iStockphoto.com/Marcela Barsse; Roasted corn © iStockphoto.com/Hugo Chang; Pinto
beans © iStockphoto.com/RedRedApple; Traditional Mexican piñata © iStockphoto.com/Joe Biafore.

Cover image: Grilled Shrimp with Avocado Butter (page 161)

We acknowledge the financial support of the Government of Canada through the Book Publishing
Industry Development Program (BPIDP) for our publishing activities.

Published by Robert Rose Inc.
120 Eglinton Avenue East, Suite 800, Toronto, Ontario, Canada M4P 1E2
Tel: (416) 322-6552 Fax: (416) 322-6936
www.robertrose.ca

Printed and bound in Canada

1 2 3 4 5 6 7 8 9 FP 21 20 19 18 17 16 15 14 13

**To Daniel and Brooke, with love and appreciation.
Cherish the celebration of family, friends and food!**

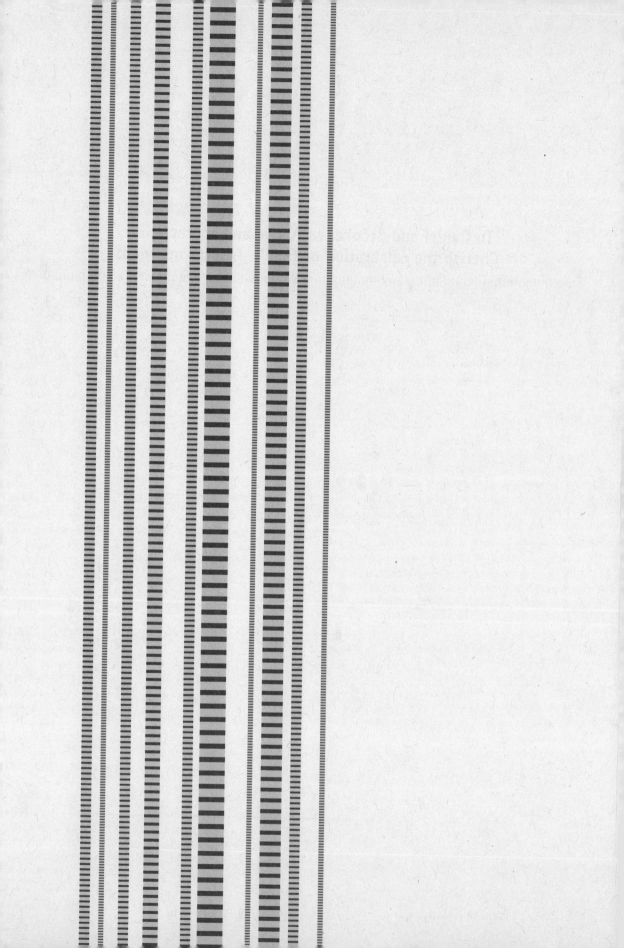

Contents

Acknowledgments

WHAT A JOY it has been this past year, cooking up the flavors of Mexico in my kitchen. How can anyone call this work? It has been a year of research, tooling around the market, grilling, baking, sautéing, chopping and tasting. As a result, this book is full of my favorite flavors collected over the past 40 years while living along the U.S.-Mexican border. Writing *200 Easy Mexican Recipes* has been a pleasure and a privilege.

This experience would not have been possible without the support of family and friends. Thank you to my son, Daniel. I enjoyed and needed your "You can do it!" attitude. To my beautiful daughter, Brooke Elizabeth, your sweet smile and heartwarming encouragement made every cooking session worthwhile. You both make me a proud mom. Roger, thank you for taking care of our daily life while I was testing, writing and tasting. Your words of encouragement and calmness kept me focused. You are all at the heart of my kitchen.

Thank you to my brothers and sister, Mike, Chris and Katie, and your families, for keeping food the focal point of our times shared with one another. To my mother and father, Fran and Ed, for lots of love, hugs, kindness and support every day.

This project was not possible without the guidance of Lisa Ekus, my literary agent. Lisa, you have remarkable vision and a guiding heart; thank you. Sally Ekus for your enthusiasm and support in keeping me connected and on track. I am also grateful to Bob Dees, who saw the potential for this book. A huge thank-you to my editor, Carol Sherman, who patiently led me through the editing process; you are incredible. To Karen Campbell-Sheviak for her copy editing and Jennifer MacKenzie for recipe testing. Thank you Daniella Zanchetta and everyone at PageWave Graphics for designing such a beautiful book, and Colin Erricson and his team for all the great photography. And to everyone who had a hand in making this book usable and inviting.

I could not have done this without the help of my dear friends and cooking pals, Leslie and Dino Cervantes and Chris Cleary. I value your culinary knowledge and thank you for testing and tasting with me. I will always be grateful. A final thank-you to Tom and Jerean Hutchinson and their amazing team at La Posta de Mesilla for their culinary expertise and inspiration.

Introduction

‖‖

I LOVE LIVING on the border!
Fortunately, I have lived along the southern border of the U.S. in Arizona, New Mexico, Texas and California. The borderland is a region where the cultures of two countries complement each other and bring about a culinary experience like no other. When I was a young girl my family moved to Southern Arizona, where I started exploring the different tastes of Mexican food, mainly Sonoran-style flavors. I discovered Traditional Chile Rellenos (page 102) and Cheese Crisps with Green Chile and Tomato (page 36) and started yearning for more. I grew up in an agricultural area around fields of fresh fruits and vegetables that were harvested daily. It was there that I learned about the Mexican culture and learned to be adventurous in my culinary world. I enjoyed guacamole (page 51) and Pico de Gallo (page 56), fresh Red Chile Tamales (page 154) and Classic Rolled Tacos (page 116). The first time I saw a frozen margarita (pages 188 to 191) was when my parents and friends were dining in Juarez Ciudad, Mexico. Ice-cold Mexican beers were ordered for the men while my mom and her friend sipped on frozen emerald green and azure blue margaritas served up in beautiful Mexican glasses. At the age of ten, I thought those fruity frozen cocktails looked like the most wonderful snow cones! My first bite of a Machaca Burritos (page 140) came after some coaxing from my adventurous brother

Chris and I enjoyed it with much delight. The first time I tried a Fresh Baja Fish Taco (page 132) I was hooked. Mexican cuisine is really about layering flavor upon flavor, adding freshness and spicy accents all at the same time. Mexican food is filled with entrées that are grilled, deep-fried, broiled or baked. They are delicious alone, incredible with sauces and melted cheese, and can be piled high with fresh produce. I love the fact that the cooking methods are so simple and basic.

In *200 Easy Mexican Recipes* I have put together a collection of recipes that will give you the basics of and foundation for good Mexican cuisine. It offers you insight on how to create the bold, complex flavors of Mexican cooking right in your own kitchen. This book is full of no-fuss recipes for authentic dishes and a fresh take on regional dishes we have come to appreciate.

Through the years I have found that good Mexican cooking is all about simplicity in methods and variety of ingredients. Simple tips like roasting a tomato before chopping can elevate the flavor of a fresh garden salsa. Try my Roasted Tomato Salsa (page 56) on any Mexican dish. Lightly grilling vegetables with chile brings together flavors that work well, as does sautéing chiles with poultry for delicious results like my Spicy Grilled Vegetables (page 159) and Pollo Verde Burritos (page 141). All of these methods add to the different levels of flavor in a Mexican kitchen.

I also like to use a combination of spices, fresh produce, cheeses and salsas in developing unforgettable flavor. Taste, texture and freshness are essential in selecting the right produce for garnishing Mexican cuisine. Be knowledgeable about the shelf life of your produce. Don't slice, tear or dice until the last minute, ensuring freshness from the field to the table. Be creative; texture and flavor can create a whole new twist on a traditional taco, burrito or a plate of enchiladas. Don't be afraid to try new types of vegetables for garnishes and salsas.

You can also get as adventurous as you want when it comes to selecting cheeses. There are so many varieties of cheese on the market that will add yet another layer of flavor to the Mexican cuisine experience. You do not need to pile it on. Just a hint of a high-quality cheese adds intense creamy flavor. The Mexican cheeses are worth a taste (see page 25). They are fresh cheeses that need no aging and are available in most Latin American markets or online.

When I had the opportunity to live in various regions of the Southwest, I noticed the coastal Mexican cuisine was lighter, included seafood and focused on a healthier version. Mexican cuisine in the northern parts of Arizona and New Mexico were influenced by the cultural flavors of area residents, while in farming communities, the chile harvests dictated the flavors served there.

Mexican cuisine has evolved into North America's comfort food. A few dishes have been Americanized, creating Tex-Mex favorites like Chile Con Queso (page 53) and Beef Fajitas (page 175). Delicious Fresh Baja Fish Tacos (page 132) and Mexican Shrimp Cocktail (page 35) are examples of Mexi-Cali cuisine that have made their way into our daily lives as well, seasoned with fresh contemporary flavor!

In *200 Easy Mexican Recipes* experience the Mexican culture through food. It's a celebration, a fiesta! In my kitchen I often look at the words inscribed above my range, *Aqui Celebramos, Familia, Amigos y Amor* — Here We Celebrate, Family, Friends and Love! My wish is that you do the same in your kitchen. *¡Buen Provecho!*

– Kelley Cleary Coffeen

History

IN THE EARLY 1500s, the Aztec's diet consisted of chiles, vegetables and corn. The earliest evidence of the tortilla was ground cornmeal that was used to make a small flatbread. Once the Spaniards arrived, they brought many cooking methods and spices to the region, which enhanced the flavors in a blending of cultures in food. The Spaniards had a deep influence on the inhabitants of Mexico. They introduced meat, poultry and pork to the indigenous people, along with methods of cooking such as roasting, steaming and grilling.

The influence of Mexican culture and food grew in the first half of this century, spilling over the border to the southwestern United States. Hispanic influences on American cooking were apparent as early as 1905 with the publication of a series of recipe books based on cooking contests held by the *Los Angeles Times* that included *Old-Time California, Spanish and Mexican Dishes... Recipes of Famous Pioneer Spanish Settlers.* That same year, H.S. Loury published *50 Choice Recipes for Spanish and Mexican Dishes.*

By the 1950s, Mexican food was gaining popularity and started becoming Americanized. The Bracero Program, a government farm worker program, brought as many as 4 million Mexican workers across the Mexican border from 1942 to 1964 into the United States to work. With them they brought the authentic flavors of Mexico and many North Americans took notice. On the Texas ranches, the Mexican workers shared their cooking methods, which led to the birth of Tex-Mex cuisine, an Americanized version of Mexican cooking. This gave way to the introduction of nachos, burritos and fajitas. Border cities such as Mexicali and Calexico were evidence that the two cultures of two nations were infused in their daily life and culinary cuisine. In the 1950s, as the fast food concept started to grow, a former marine with a passion for Mexican food started selling 19-cent tacos at his small family restaurant in California. Eventually, in the early '60s, Glen Bell established the first franchised Mexican fast food restaurant, known as Taco Bell. This chain of restaurants gave national recognition to Mexican food for the first time.

The Hispanic population increased over the next few decades, bringing a new appreciation for Mexican cuisine. Texas, New Mexico, Arizona and parts of California and Florida are home to a high Mexican/Hispanic population, leading to a wide variety of authentic Mexican restaurants. In more recent years, notable authors such as Diane Kennedy and Rick Bayless embraced the authentic flavors of Mexico and offered a distinction from Americanized Mexican foods. Whether it is authentic Mexican, Tex-Mex, Cal-Mex or New Mex, it is a true passion for those who prepare it, from neighborhood line cooks to high-end chefs and TV food personalities, and those of us who crave it. We now celebrate Mexican holidays such as Cinco de Mayo (May 5th) and others as if they were our own. It has become a part of our culture — an ethnic comfort food that speaks to the world.

Mexican Cuisine Essentials

Tools and Equipment

Tortilla press

Tortilla presses are available in cast iron that is polished to a chrome finish. This simple kitchen tool has a base, top and handle. It is great for not only pressing out tortillas but also making the perfect dough for tartlets or empanadas. Moist balls of flour tortilla dough or corn masa are placed in the center of the press and then pressed to a thin layer for tortillas or pastries. I use a press to create the perfect corn and flour tortillas.

Tortilla warmer

These small insulated tortilla warmers with lids are decorative and useful for keeping the tortillas warm. They are available in colorful ceramic styles as well as plastic — polyethylene material that keeps fresh tortillas hot. Also fabric tortilla warmers that can be heated in the microwave are available in an array of colors.

Kitchen shears

I use kitchen shears to trim store-bought flour tortillas to a smaller size. It is difficult to find 6-inch (15 cm) flour tortillas, which are the perfect size for many tacos. I trim the 8- or 10-inch (20 to 25 cm) tortilla to a 6-inch (15 cm) size with shears.

Skillet

A large 10- to 12-inch (25 to 30 cm) nonstick heavy skillet that is at least 2-inches (5 cm) deep is perfect for sautéing meats, veggies, chicken or fish, and also pan searing meats.

Deep fryer

Look for deep-fry sets that include a base, a nonstick pot and basket with a handle. It should heat to at least 375°F (190°C). I prefer an electric deep fryer that has a rectangular shape with a large pot that holds 10 to 12 cups (2.5 to 3 L) of oil and a mesh basket with a heat-resistant handle. You will be frying tostada shells, chimichangas, and tacos that are generally 6- to 8-inches (15 to 20 cm) long, making the rectangular basket ideal. There are also round fryers available but they limit how many tacos you can cook at one time.

Thermometers
Digital instant-read thermometer

This is a simple tool that is a necessity for checking the internal temperature of larger pieces of meat and poultry. The oven-safe type can be set to the exact temperature you want. An alarm sounds when the desired temperature is achieved. Some thermometers cannot be put directly in the oven but can measure the temperature by probing the roast once removed from the grill or oven.

Candy/deep-fry thermometer

This thermometer is needed for checking the temperature of oil when deep-frying churros, sopapillas, chimichangas and tacos. It records temperatures from 100 to 400°F (38 to 200°C). It is approximately 12 inches (30 cm) long and clips to the side of the pot for safety.

Grills

Selecting a barbecue grill is a very personal choice. Some people like grilling with gas, others prefer the traditional charcoal grills and still others prefer grilling with wood. A barbecue grill is perfect for grilling meats, fish, poultry and vegetables. Small thin pieces of meat, fish and vegetables cook quickly and are well suited to grilling at high heat levels. However, larger pieces of meat, poultry and fish can be grilled to perfection at lower heat levels. Grilling is a quick and perfect cooking method for many beef, chicken and fish entrees.

Gas grill

Gas grilling is flame cooking with temperatures of up to 600°F (315°C). Gas grills are quick and convenient, with push button ignition systems. They generally have 2 or 3 cooking zones so you can find the right temperature when cooking. Propane adds no flavor as it burns.

Charcoal grill

These grills burn hotter and dryer than propane or gas grills. This causes the high, dry heat of the charcoal to sear the meat more quickly. The high, dry heat caramelizes the proteins in the meat and fish and caramelizes the plant sugars in vegetables and fruits. You can also add wood chunks to charcoal to add a wood flavor to your meats or fish.

Indoor grill

When outdoor grilling is not an option, indoor grills work nicely. There are a wide variety of indoor electric grills. Small, thin pieces of meat, fish and vegetables cook quickly and are well suited to an indoor grill. Indoor grills are quick to heat up and easy to clean. You may not get all of the authentic flavors of outdoor grilling, but you can compensate for that by using spices, glazes and marinades. There are open grills and contact grills, some large, some small. There are many online resources that review grills. Do some research and find the right grilling method and grill for you.

Grilling mitts

Heat resistant, with a long, form-fitting cuff that gives you protection when grilling or deep-frying (see also Heat-resistant kitchen gloves or mitts, right).

Tongs

A long and a short pair is helpful in deep-frying and grilling. Use the long pair of tongs for deep-frying in order to keep your hands and arms away from the hot oil.

Heat-resistant kitchen gloves or mitts

Keeps hands and arms safe when deep-frying and grilling. Look for mitts made with a heat-resistant fiber and nonslip silicone grip. These are generally good for heat up to 400°F (200°C). I like both mitts and gloves. Gloves allow the use of your fingers for more control. You can find these online or in most kitchen supply stores (see also Grilling mitts, left).

Cutting boards

I like to have several cutting boards on hand. An antibacterial cutting board for raw meats, fish and chicken and a couple of favorite wood boards for veggies and cheeses.

Cheese grater

I like to grate and shred my own cheese when I can. A lot of bulk cheeses seem to have more flavor than pre-shredded varieties. Most of the Mexican cheeses will come in bulk form.

Ice cream scooper

I like to create the perfect scoop for my Mexican Sundae (page 208). I find that the ice cream scoopers with the thumb trigger are sometimes difficult to use. But if you use that type, look for one that holds ½ cup (125 mL). I prefer the old-fashioned aluminum scoopers. You can work the ice cream into a perfect ball with ease.

Heavy-duty foil

Heavy-duty foil, as opposed to regular foil, is perfect for creating molds for shaping taco shells (see page 118). The heaviness creates and holds the perfect shape that will withstand the heat of hot oil when deep-frying.

Dry measuring cups

Use plastic or metal measuring cups with flat rims to measure dry ingredients such as flour, sugar, beans and corn masa. They come in graduated sizes ranging from ¼ cup (60 mL) to 1 cup (250 mL). Spoon dry ingredients into the appropriate size cup and level off with the flat side of a knife or spatula. I also use these measuring cups to measure chopped vegetables and cheeses.

Liquid measuring cups

Use standard glass or Pyrex measuring cups with spouts to measure water, oil, milk and juice. Place the cup on a flat surface and add liquid until the desired measurement is reached, bending over while pouring so your eye is level with the measure. There are also angled liquid measuring cups that have the measurement line on the inside of the cup. You can measure without bending over to view the measurement.

Whisks

Use a sturdy whisk for sauces, creams, eggs and fillings in order to get well blended results.

Small whisk — select a small whisk for eggs, sauces and marinades. I also use this for mixing spices for rubs.

Large whisk — use a larger whisk for batters, tempuras and cream fillings. If you only buy one whisk select a sturdy medium whisk, which will work for both.

Mixing bowls

A nested set of glass or ceramic mixing bowls will be used quite often. I use small or medium bowls for marinades, salsas, sauces and tossing spices together. I use large bowls for tossing mixed greens, whipping cream fillings and mixing tortilla dough.

Small serving bowls

When serving "family style" it is nice to have a group of small matching bowls (6 to 10 oz/175 to 300 g) for tostada, enchilada, burrito and taco garnishes, cheeses and salsas. I use small glass or Pyrex bowls for fresh herbs and spices. I also have a set of brightly colored ceramic bowls that make the condiments look more festive.

Small chafing dish

I use a 5-quart chafing dish for entertaining and serving "family style." I use them to keep tortillas, taco and burrito fillings and queso warm. There are a variety of styles and sizes on the market. You can find electric or Sterno-style (Sterno flame disposable burners) chafing dishes ranging from 4 to 5 quarts.

Hand-held citrus juicer

I use a lot of fresh citrus juice in my salsas and sauces. I also like to accent grilled meats, chicken and fish with fresh lemon and lime juice. A hand-held juicer comes in handy for a quick zest of flavor. You can find heavy plastic ones in bright, fun colors. They also come in aluminum and other metals.

Zester

A Microplane grater is sharp with a fine grate that is perfect for citrus. It makes adding a bit of zest from limes, lemons and oranges to sauces and salsas quick and easy.

Ingredient Essentials

The ingredients in this book make some assumptions about what is standard when it comes to basic ingredients. For the best results, follow the recipe and use the recommended ingredient, unless other options are indicated in a tip or variation. Here is a list of what is assumed:

- All eggs used are large eggs.
- 2% milk and yogurt unless otherwise specified.
- Butter is salted unless otherwise specified.
- Fresh vegetables and fruits are medium-size unless otherwise indicated. Any inedible peels, skins, seeds and cores are removed unless otherwise indicated.
- "Onions" means regular cooking onions unless otherwise indicated.
- "Mushrooms" means white button mushrooms unless otherwise indicated.
- With canned tomatoes and tomato products, the juice is also used unless the recipe instructs you to drain it.
- When broth (chicken, beef or vegetable) is called for, homemade is the ideal, but ready-to-use broth in Tetra Paks comes a close second. If you can only find canned broth, make sure to dilute it as directed on the can before use.
- Canned soups are used undiluted unless otherwise specified.
- Chopped or minced garlic is freshly chopped or minced, not purchased already minced and preserved.

Common Ingredients

Tortillas

Tortillas are available in corn and flour. Handmade tortillas are delicious and easy to make (see pages 70 to 73). Store-bought or fresh tortillas made at your local tortilla factory also work well. The key to good Mexican food is to use the freshest tortillas possible and warm them before using so they are pliable. Available in 4-, 6-, 8-, 10- and 12-inch (10, 15, 20, 25 and 30 cm) sizes.

Corn tortillas

Corn tortillas are round thin flatbreads made from masa harina or corn flour. They average about 40 calories, less than 1 gram of fat and about 12 grams of carbohydrates. You can buy yellow, white and blue corn tortillas. Blue corn has more protein and less starch than white corn. Corn tortillas can be frozen in an airtight container and defrosted and reheated when ready to use.

Flour tortillas

Flour tortillas are round thin unleavened Mexican flatbreads, made from wheat flour. There is an increasing variety of tortillas on the market, from whole wheat and multigrain to fat-free and carb-balanced. Flavored tortillas such as spinach herb, jalapeño, Cheddar, sun-dried tomato and garlic herb are just a few of the varieties available. Sizes generally range from 4- to 12-inches (10 to 30 cm). Flour tortillas can be frozen in an airtight container and defrosted and reheated when ready to use.

Flour

You can make tortillas with all-purpose or whole wheat flour or a combination of both.

Masa harina

A dry form of corn, masa is made from white corn that has been treated with mineral lime and then stone ground. It is used to make fresh corn tortillas and tamales.

Oils

Peanut oil

I like to use organic oil derived from peanuts. It's perfect for deep-frying corn tortilla chips, tacos, tostada and taco shells, chimichangas and sopapillas because it has a high-smoke point. They fry faster and seem to be crispier.

Vegetable oil

This oil is very versatile. It adds no taste or flavor to foods. It works well for deep-frying tacos, taco shells, corn tortilla chips, etc. I use vegetable oil for sautéing meats and vegetables when I do not want to add additional flavor.

Olive oil

Derived from olives, this oil has health benefits and adds a nice hint of flavor to sautéed meats and vegetables. Its flavors are added to salsas and sauces as well. Olive oils range in flavor from mild and extra light to bold, rich and fruity. I use the bolder flavors when sautéing with garlic and onion and the lighter flavors when adding to sauces, marinades and salsas.

Nonstick cooking spray

I use nonstick cooking spray for a variety of cooking techniques. I coat meat, chicken or fish surface with cooking spray so the spices will stick to it before roasting or grilling and no extra flavor will be added. For some tacos shells and wraps, I spray the corn and flour tortillas lightly before skillet warming for a lightly toasted texture. There are quite a few flavored sprays such as olive oil and butter. Test them out and see what you prefer. I also use cooking spray to coat skillets and baking sheets. Look for the cooking spray specifically for grilling to coat your barbecue grill.

Chiles

Chipotle chile in adobo sauce

Dried jalapeños marinated in a smoky sauce made of onions, tomato and garlic. It is generally canned and is available in the Mexican food section at the market.

Dried red chile pods

Usually rehydrated and blended and used in sauces. Available in plastic bags in the Mexican food section at the market.

Habanero

Small and orange. Known as one of the hottest chiles in the world. Available fresh in the produce section at the market.

Jalapeño

Small bright green chile. They range from mild to hot, used in salsas, sauces and many Mexican dishes. Available fresh in the produce section at the market.

Pickled jalapeños

Small bright green chile, marinated in an oil, vinegar and herb solution. Available canned or bottled in the Mexican food or condiment section at the market.

New Mexico or Anaheim

Long thin green chile pepper with medium to hot varieties. Used in salsas and sauces. Tastes best when roasted, seeded and peeled (see page 98).

Available fresh in the produce section of the market. Regional crops are in season during the early fall months but imports are available most of the year. Roasted green chile can also be found in most frozen food sections at the market or online.

Poblano

Larger green chile used in salsas and sauces. Rich, earthy flavor, mild to medium in heat. Tastes best when roasted, seeded and peeled. Available fresh in the produce section of the market.

Serrano

Small thin green chile, usually hotter than a jalapeño. Available fresh in the produce section of the market.

Yellow chile

Yellow, waxy appearance, mild in flavor. Available fresh in the produce section of the market.

Vegetables

Avocados

This vegetable has a creamy texture and exceptional nutrients, including antioxidants. It adds a natural buttery flavor when used as a garnish.

Bell peppers

Large peppers that are mild in taste. There is no heat in their flavor. Red bells are sweeter than the green or orange.

Cabbage

Cabbage comes in red and green varieties. This fresh vegetable makes the perfect garnish and is available year round. These two types of cabbage add color and texture to my Festive Mexican Slaw (page 107) or garnish for tostadas, tacos, enchiladas, burritos and chimichangas. I like to use red when I think I need more color in my taco recipe. For example a white fish with a white sauce needs a splash of color like my Fresh Baja Fish Tacos (page 132). So I add Pico de Gallo (page 56) and red and green cabbage.

Corn

This vegetable is a good source of B vitamins and adds fiber to the diet. It has a hint of sweetness and blends well with chile in salsas.

Garlic

Garlic is a pungent bulb that has a sharp and strong flavor. It adds a depth of flavor to sautéed fillings, marinades, sauces and salsas.

Green onions

These little onions, also known as scallions, add a sharp flavor to tacos and salsas. The crunchy texture makes them good to use as a garnish.

Lettuces

Iceberg lettuce

This lettuce is mild in flavor but the crunchy texture adds a refreshing garnish to tostadas, tacos, tortas and Tostaditos (page 48).

Romaine

This leafy green lettuce adds a lot of color along with texture as a garnish for my tacos, tostadas, burritos and chimichangas. I love it in my Chopped Mexican Salad (page 108).

Salad mix

There are a variety of salad mixes with a wide range of flavors on the market. There are red and green lettuce varieties that range in taste from intense bittery spice to sweet and mild. "Living" lettuce and "artisan" lettuce and greens are also available. Many are available prewashed and packaged in your produce section. Taste and compare to find your favorite combination of greens.

Jicama

Jicama is a Mexican root plant that is creamy white with a crisp, distinctive texture. It is mild in taste and adds texture to salsas and fillings.

Onions

Onions are available in yellow, white and red varieties. They vary in taste and flavor. Look for mild-tasting onions, such as white onions, to blend with chile and add to salsas. If you are looking to sweeten a sauce or salsa, use red onions, or onions specifically labeled "sweet onions." They will add a bit of a sweet flavor to your recipes.

Potato

This versatile root vegetable can take on other flavors and works well in taco fillings, Mexican soups and side dishes with red and green chiles. I use a basic russet potato. However, experiment with golden potatoes for a more buttery flavor or new potatoes for a fresher, sweeter flavor.

Spinach

This leafy green is high in choline and folic acid and is an appetizing garnish for tostadas, tacos, tortas and burritos. I team fresh spinach with a variety of meats, vegetables, cheeses and seafood for a delicious garnish.

Tomatoes, fresh and canned

Fresh and canned are both perfect for fresh salsas, enhancing the flavorful chile and spices. I like ripe greenhouse tomatoes for fresh vegetables salsas, Pico de Gallo and as a garnish for enchiladas, tostadas, tacos, burritos, chimichangas, nachos and enchiladas. I use canned tomatoes in cooking sauces and stews. Canned tomatoes are convenient and easy to keep on hand. There is a growing variety of flavors offered in canned tomatoes, such as roasted garlic, balsamic, basil and oil, and green pepper, celery and onions. An unflavored canned diced tomato works best unless otherwise noted.

Tomatillos

A small green tomato-like fruit covered in a green filmy husk. It has a citrusy flavor and is perfect for sauces and salsas.

Zucchini

This vegetable can be eaten raw or cooked. I use it sautéed in side dishes and taco fillings and uncooked for garnishes and in salsas.

Fruits

Apples

A fruit that adds a natural sweetness, fiber and texture to salsas and sauces. I like the sweet-sour tartness of Golden and Delicious apples along with Granny Smith.

Blueberries

Blueberries are indigo colored berries with a sweet flavor.

Lemons

A citrusy fruit high in vitamin C and limonene. It adds a sharp taste and complements vegetable and fruit combinations in taco toppings and sweet and savory salsas. Adding a zest of the lemon rind to salsas and sauces adds another hint of fresh flavor. Juicing a fresh lemon generally yields about 2 to 3 tbsp (30 to 45 mL) of fresh juice. Roll a room temperature lemon on the counter a few times to maximize the amount of juice. Fresh lemon juice has a lighter, zestier flavor than bottled juice.

Limes

A fruit high in vitamin C that adds refreshing citrusy flavor to vegetable toppings and salsas. Heightens the taste of chile. Freshly squeezed lime juice has a fresher, lighter taste than bottled juice. Zesting the rind of a lime for salsas and sauces adds flavor and color.

Mangos

A fruit high in vitamin A. It has a sweet pineapple-banana flavor. The texture is smooth and velvety. Select a mango that is firm yet just soft to the touch.

Oranges

Orange is a citrus fruit high in vitamin C and limonene. It is citrusy, yet sweeter than lemons and limes. Adds flavor to marinades for meats and sauces and makes a good sweet salsa.

Pineapple

A fruit high in vitamin C. It is a very sweet fruit with good texture for sweet salsas. It blends well with a variety of chile peppers. You can use fresh or canned pineapple. Canned pineapple can be a bit sweeter and more consistent than fresh pineapple. There are a variety of cuts available in canned pineapple, such as chunky, tidbits, rings and crushed. Drain if directed in recipe. A fresh pineapple needs to have the skin removed and the center removed, then cut to desired size chunks.

Raspberries

Raspberries are a red berry that have a textured surface and a sweet-tart flavor.

Legumes and Grains

Black beans

Black, shiny kidney-shaped beans with an earthy flavor. They blend well with meats and cook well in stews. You can use dry or canned. Dried black beans are best cooked like pinto beans (page 99). The canned beans are nice and firm and should be rinsed before using.

Pinto beans

Pinto beans are a fat-free, high-protein legume that adds fiber to the Mexican meal as a side dish or in taco, burrito, tostada and chimichanga fillings. After being cooked (page 99) they can be smashed and reheated for a popular refried bean filling (page 100). Canned pinto beans are a convenient choice and have good flavor and texture.

Red beans

Also known as kidney beans. They have a good texture and rich flavor when cooked. Canned kidney beans are widely available. They are a bit softer but work well in taco and burrito fillings.

Rice

Cooked rice adds fiber and taste to taco, burrito and chimichanga fillings. It is also an economical way to expand the volume of taco fillings. It lends itself to herbs, spices and flavorings and makes a wonderful side dish. Brown rice is very nutritious and can be used as a healthier option. White long-grain rice is more prevalent in Mexican food. It is longer and stays separate, allowing each grain to grab and hold flavors and spices. Short-grain rice is a moister round grain that does not work as well in these Mexican fillings. However, it can be used as a side dish with herbs and spices.

Herbs and Spices

Herbs

Cilantro

A green flat-leaf herb that has a distinctive pungent flavor. It is used widely in Mexican cuisine, especially as a garnish and in salsas.

Italian flat-leaf parsley

This is a mild herb that adds color and texture to marinades and sauces.

Mexican oregano

Stronger in flavor and different in texture than regular oregano. It is delicious in soups, stews and sauces.

Spices

Cayenne pepper

This is a chile powder that has a hot edgy flavor to it. It spices up sauces, stews and salsas.

Cinnamon

This is a fragrant spice that blends well with fruits and chocolate. It has a spicy clove flavor to it.

Cumin

Earthy, nutty flavor and aroma. Just a pinch adds flavor to sauces and marinades.

Hot pepper flakes

These flakes come from hot dried red peppers and add heat to salsas, marinades and sauces.

Seasonings and Blends

Garlic and herb seasoning

Dry garlic and herb blends vary in taste and flavor combinations. Some blends combine up to 20 spices and herbs. Try a few and find your favorite.

Italian seasoning

A combination of dry herbs and spices such as basil, marjoram, oregano and sage.

Cheese Varieties

Soft cheese

Cream cheese is a mild soft white cheese make from cow's cream and milk. Whipped cream cheese, which is a favorite of mine, has air whipped into it. It is easy to use and does not need to be softened.

Semisoft cheese

Feta cheese has a texture that can range from soft to semisoft. It is a brined curd white cheese with a crumbly texture and is traditionally made in Greece.

Panela and Queso Fresco are fresh cheeses with a crumbly texture that taste like a combination of Monterey Jack and mozzarella cheese. Their main characteristic is that they do not melt, but will get soft when warmed. They are mild and differ in taste slightly, but add a lightly salted cheese flavor when used as a garnish for tacos, burritos, beans, casseroles and more.

Semifirm cheese

Cheddar is a semifirm cow's milk cheese that originated in England. Its flavor ranges from mild to sharp depending on the length of aging.

Monterey Jack is an American semifirm cheese that has creamy mild flavor and is white in color. It is a melting cheese.

Swiss cheese is white in color with holes in its texture. It has a mild, buttery, almost fruit-like flavor.

Hard cheese

Anejo enchilado is a firm Mexican aged (anejo means "aged") cheese that is rolled in paprika. It is used as a stuffing or topping for enchiladas, burritos or tacos.

Cotija is a hard Mexican cow's milk cheese, originating in the Mexican town of Cotija. It has a strong flavor and grating properties from its dry crumbly texture. This cheese is salted and then aged for up to one year. It's used to garnish and top tacos, adding a flavorful garnish to Mexican dishes. It's also used to mix in directly with other ingredients to enhance the flavor. It is tagged as the Parmesan of Mexico. Parmesan is a dense hard Italian cheese that is dry and sharp. It is aged for two or more years. It has a sharp, pungent flavor.

Blue cheese

Blue cheese is a crumbly white cheese that is visibly marbled with blue-green mold. It has a tart, sharp flavor.

Melting cheese

Asadero, Queso Blanco, Queso Quesadilla and Manchego cheeses are among many cheeses that melt easily and are used in quesadillas and many Mexican recipes due to their creamy and rich elements. Asadero cheese has a smooth texture, is yellow in color and has a tangy yet mild flavor. Queso Blanco and Queso Quesadilla cheeses are mild in flavor and white in color. Manchego is a buttery yellow cheese with a salty, nutty flavor.

Toppings

Salsas and Sauces

Salsas and sauces are the simplest way of heightening the flavor of any Mexican dish. Multiple combinations of tomato, chile peppers and onions add a ton of flavor and variety to this cuisine. Salsas and sauces can also be the crowning moment, the last chance for culinary inspiration. After we have warmed our fresh tortillas, scooped up our taco or burrito or torta filling and layered fresh greens and veggies on top, it is time to lavish our hand-held creation with an exquisite tasting salsa or sauce. A well-made salsa will elevate the combination of flavors in even the best-made burritos, enchiladas, tortas and rellenos. Gone are the days when there were only a few salsas to choose from. We have moved on to explore all the opportunities that fresh vegetables, herbs, chile and fruits can give the salsa world.

There are relish-style salsas that are big on texture, such as Pico de Gallo (page 56), Green Chile Relish (page 61), Garlic and Jalapeño Relish (page 62), and some that are roasted and smoked like Roasted Tomato Salsa (page 56).

There are herb salsas with intense flavor that are easy to make with a few ingredients, such as Salsa Verde (page 58). Rich hot sauces make a lasting impression with their intense level of savory flavors and heat. Try my Red Enchilada Sauce (page 63), Green Enchilada Sauce (page 64) and Quick Mole Sauce (page 68). Fruit salsas like Citrus Salsa (page 59) are refreshing and tangy. Speaking of tangy, the flavor of a tomatillo leaves that hint of citrus flavor in my Tomatillo Avocado Salsa (page 60).

A new trend is dairy sauces made from fresh yogurt and sour cream, which can add delightful highlights to a fresh fish taco. It has become a favorite finishing touch. The collection of recipes in the Salsas, Relishes and Sauces chapter will enliven the flavor of Mexican entrées. So enjoy, and surprise your taste buds with new adventures and flavor combinations.

Fresh Vegetables

Burritos, tacos, tortas and enchiladas can be adorned with a variety of fresh garnishes, from the familiar flavors of diced tomato, chopped onion and shredded iceberg lettuce to the extraordinary taste and textures of jicama, pineapple and tomatillos.

Taste, texture and freshness are the key elements in selecting the garnish for any Mexican entree. Buy good-quality vegetables at the very last minute to ensure freshness and taste. Fresh vegetables lend themselves to the light and healthy characteristics of a fish or seafood taco. Rich flavors from avocados and the sharpness of a fresh onion heighten the taste of a beefy taco or cheesy enchilada or add extra texture and flavor to a shredded chicken tostada.

I like lots of fresh greens, chopped or shredded, on many of my tortas and burrito bowls. Investigate the varieties of salad mix and greens in your produce department. Look for interesting, unusual vegetables and greens. Try a few fresh herbs as well. Fresh cilantro, chives or basil are delightful thrown in with a chopped salad mix.

Cheese

Cheese is an important part of Mexican cuisine. Cheddar and Monterey Jack cheeses are two of the most popular choices. But traditionally the authentic tacos, tostadas and tortas of Mexico are garnished with a hint of cheese. Even though they have a shorter shelf life than American or European cheeses, I encourage you to explore the cheeses of Mexico, such as Cotija, Asadero and Queso Fresco. The Mexican cheeses are worth every ounce of cream. These fresh cheeses, melting cheeses or hard/semifirm cheeses are readily available in most markets. A creamy cheese, such as Asadero, can be melted inside a warm taco, while a fresh cheese, such as Queso Fresco can be crumbled and sprinkled on top of garnishes. The firmer cheeses like Cotija add intense pungent flavors and a little goes a long way (see also Cheese Varieties, page 23).

Not all Mexican entrées need cheese. Many can stand with only garnishes and salsa. However, additions of Cheddar, Monterey Jack, hints of blue cheese, feta and, of course, the Mexican ones, add unmatched flavor to the Mexican entrée.

Mexican Food Definitions

Adobo sauce: A smoky chile-based sauce most often made with garlic, vinegar and chile peppers.

Agua Fresca: A fresh water drink infused with fruits, spices and seeds that is very popular in Mexico.

Albondigas: Mexican meatball soup.

Anaheim chile: see Chiles (page 19).

Antojitos: A Mexican street snack that means "little whims" or "craving." It is an appetizer or small portion of something.

Bolillos: A popular Mexican yeast roll.

Caldillo: Beef and vegetable soup.

Carne: Refers to meats, such as pork and beef.

Carne asada: Means "roasted meat," most-often meat cooked over coals.

Carnitas: Means "little meats" and refers to a simmered pork filling for tacos or burritos.

Ceviche: Raw fish marinated in lime juice accompanied by diced chile, tomato and onion.

Chavela: Spicy beer cocktail.

Chile rellenos: A large green chile pepper, such as Anahiem or New Mexico, stuffed with cheese, then dipped in an egg batter and lightly fried.

Chipotle: see Chiles (page 19).

Cilantro: see Herbs (page 23).

Corn masa: A dough of ground cornmeal, lime and water, used to make corn tortillas.

Corn masa harina: see Masa harina (page 18).

Cotija: see Cheese (page 23).

Crispy folded taco: A corn or flour tortilla deep-fried in the shape of a "U" and filled with taco filling of either beef, chicken, fish or veggies.

Cupitas: Mexican slang for small crispy, corn or flour tortillas shaped into a cup form.

Dulce: Means "sweet" and refers to sweets or candy.

Elote: The Mexican name for fresh corn on the cob.

Empanada: A pastry turnover filled with spicy meat or fruit.

Enchilada: A lightly fried corn or flour tortilla dipped in red or green chile sauce and filled with either cheese, meat or chicken and rolled.

Escabeche: A mixture of oil, vinegar and herbs used to pickle jalapeños, onions and carrots.

Fajita: A traditional Tex-Mex dish of grilled beef, chicken or shrimp, sliced and served with grilled onions and peppers. It is served with fresh tortillas and garnishes on the side. Once served the filling is then placed into the tortillas and garnished with fresh produce.

Flan: A custard-style dessert.

Flauta: A flour tortilla filled with chicken, beef or beans and rolled and deep-fried.

Folded taco: Flour or corn tortilla folded in half and stuffed with filling. The tortilla can be soft or crispy.

Frijoles: Dried beans. Rijoles refritos refers to refried beans (see also Refried Beans).

Guacamole: A creamy dip or garnish made with mashed avocado, onions, chiles, tomato and lime juice.

Habanero chile: see Chiles (page 19).

Horchata: Cinnamon rice milk.

Huevos: Spanish for "eggs."

Jicama: see Vegetables (page 19).

Leche: Spanish for "milk."

Mexican Chocolate: A hard chocolate with a rough and gritty texture that is a combination of cocoa, sugar and cinnamon.

Mexican chorizo: A locally made fresh sausage with red chiles and pork.

Menudo: Mildly flavored tripe soup.

Nachitos: Mexican slang for mini nachos. Nachos are a Mexican appetizer of crispy tortilla chips covered in melted cheese and topped with a jalapeño slice.

Posole: A pork and hominy soup. Served during the holiday season.

Quesadilla: A flour or corn tortilla stuffed with cheese and grilled until the cheese is melted.

Queso: Spanish for "cheese." Referred to as melted cheese.

Refried beans: Cooked and mashed pinto beans sauteed or "refried" with oil or lard.

Rolled taco: A 6-inch (15 cm) corn tortilla filled either with chicken, beef or beans, then rolled and deep-fried.

Salsa: A condiment made of a combination of vegetables, fruits and chiles, served with chips or over Mexican dishes.

Sangria: Spanish wine punch made with brandy, red wine, liqueur and fresh fruit.

Sangrita: Tequila chaser made of tomato and citrus flavors.

Sopapilla: A light pastry that is deep-fried and typically hollow in the center.

Tamale: A meat filling wrapped in a masa and steamed in a corn husk.

Taquito: Miniature rolled tacos.

Tequila: A liquor originating in Mexico made of distilled juice of the agave plant and named for the town Tequila, Jalisco, Mexico. It is popular in margaritas, and the finer tequilas are served as a sipping tequila.

Tomatillo: see Vegetables (page 19).

Torta: A Mexican sandwich with grilled meats or poultry garnished with cheese, guacamole and pico de gallo served on a bolillo or large bun.

Appetizers

Authentic Mexican Bean Dip

Makes 3 cups (750 mL)	

This is a flavorful dip that starts with a basic refritos frijoles (well-fried beans). You can customize this dip for an appetizer everyone will love, such as adding jalapeños, a bit of onion and topping with a flavorful Mexican cheese.

- Preheat oven to 275°F (140°C)
- Food processor
- Ovenproof serving bowl

3	jalapeño peppers, seeded and chopped	3
2	cans (each 14 to 19 oz/398 to 540 mL) pinto beans, drained, liquid reserved	2
2 tbsp	lard (see Tips, right)	30 mL
Pinch	garlic powder	Pinch
	Salt	
1 cup	shredded Monterey Jack cheese	250 mL
	Tortilla chips	
	Salsa	

1. Place jalapeños in a small saucepan and cover with 1 inch (2.5 cm) water. Bring to boil over high heat and boil until jalapeños are soft, 4 to 5 minutes. Drain and let cool slightly.

2. Transfer drained jalapeños to a food processor and process until smooth. Set aside.

3. In a large skillet, combine beans and ¼ cup (60 mL) reserved liquid and bring to a boil over medium-high heat and boil, stirring occasionally, for 2 minutes. Reduce heat to low. Using a potato masher, gently mash beans. Beans should be like a thick paste, not runny. If too thick, add more reserved liquid, 1 tsp (5 mL) at a time, until bean mixture is thick but not stiff. Repeat until all beans are mashed. Remove from heat. Transfer to a bowl.

Tips

If you are pressed for time, instead of heating beans in a skillet in Step 3, place beans and liquid, in 2-cup (500 mL) increments, into a food processor and pulse for 5 minutes until a smooth but lumpy texture. Be careful not to overprocess. Continue with Step 4. Pour into an ovenproof serving bowl.

Substitute 2 tbsp (30 mL) vegetable or canola oil for the lard.

4. Add lard to skillet and melt over medium-high heat. Add mashed beans and cook, stirring, until well blended and bubbly, 4 to 6 minutes. Stir in jalapeño purée and garlic powder and season with salt to taste. Place in an ovenproof dish and top with cheese.

5. Bake in preheated oven until cheese is melted, 8 to 10 minutes. Serve with tortilla chips and salsa.

Variation

Chorizo Bean Dip: After completing Step 2, in a large skillet over medium heat, cook 10 oz (300 g) fresh chorizo, removed from casings and breaking up with a spoon, until meat is cooked through, 4 to 5 minutes. Transfer to paper towels to drain. Wipe out skillet and proceed with Step 3. Spread bean mixture into bowl as directed, then spread chorizo over top and sprinkle with cheese. Proceed with Step 5.

Fresh Tortilla Chips

Freshly made tortilla chips and a big bowl of salsa are the essence of Mexican cuisine. These crispy fried chips made with either corn or flour tortillas elevate the flavor of any Mexican salsa or appetizer.

Tips

For deep-frying, I prefer to use peanut oil because it has a higher smoke point. Canola oil and vegetable oil are good oils to use as well.

You can make these chips ahead and store in an airtight container for up to 2 days.

- Candy/deep-fry thermometer

	Oil (see Tips, left)	
6	6-inch (15 cm) corn or 8-inch (20 cm) flour tortillas, each cut into 6 wedges	6
	Salt, optional	

1. Fill a deep fryer, deep heavy pot or deep skillet with 3 inches (7.5 cm) of oil and heat to 350°F (180°C). Using tongs, gently place 4 to 6 tortilla wedges at a time in the hot oil and deep-fry, turning once, until crisp, 1 to 2 minutes. Drain on paper towels. Salt to taste. Serve chips warm or at room temperature.

Variation

Oven-Baked Chips: Preheat oven to 400°F (200°C). Lightly spray tortilla wedges with cooking spray. Place on a baking sheet and bake until golden brown, 6 to 8 minutes per side. Remove and serve immediately or let cool.

Mexican Shrimp Cocktail

Makes 4 to 6 servings

Enjoy this saucy Mexican-style shrimp cocktail. It's a little thinner than a regular cocktail sauce, with a spicy twist. Fresh avocado accents this tangy, refreshing cocktail.

16 to 24	medium shrimp, peeled and deveined	16 to 24
1 cup	finely chopped celery	250 mL
3	green onions, green parts only, chopped	3
2 tbsp	minced cilantro	30 mL
1	tomato, seeded and chopped	1
3 cups	spicy vegetable juice cocktail	750 mL
½ cup	picante salsa	125 mL
	Juice of 2 limes	
	Salt and freshly ground black pepper	
2	avocados	2

1. In a large pot of boiling water, boil shrimp until opaque and pink, about 2 minutes. Drain and let cool slightly. Peel and discard shells. Place shrimp in a bowl, cover and refrigerate until chilled, for at least 30 minutes or for up to 2 hours.

2. In a large bowl, combine celery, green onions, cilantro, tomato, vegetable juice and salsa. Add shrimp and lime juice and mix well. Season with salt and pepper to taste. Just before serving, dice avocado and add to mixture. Serve in decorative glassware.

Variation

For a thicker and richer flavor, add 1 cucumber, peeled, seeded and finely diced in Step 2.

Cheese Crisps with Green Chile and Tomato

Makes 6 slices

Cheese crisps are simply a toasted flour tortilla topped with melted cheese and a bit of chile. It is the hint of butter that brings these flavors together. This Sonoran-style favorite has a distinct flavor that reminds me of growing up on the border. Enjoy this simple appetizer that will melt in your mouth.

● Preheat broiler with rack 3 to 4 inches (7.5 to 10 cm) from heat

1	10- to 12-inch (25 to 30 cm) flour tortilla	1
1 tbsp	butter, at room temperature	15 mL
6 oz	Cheddar cheese, shredded	175 g
2 tbsp	diced seeded tomato	30 mL
2 tbsp	roasted green chile peppers (see page 98)	30 mL

1. Spread one side of tortilla with butter, spreading it evenly to edges of tortilla. Place tortilla on a baking sheet and top with cheese, tomato and chile.

2. Broil cheese crisp until cheese is melted and tortilla is crispy around the edges and slightly brown, 1 to 2 minutes. Slice into 6 wedges.

Variation
Omit tomato and chile.

Mexican Shrimp Shooters

|||||||||||||||||||||||||||||||||||||||||||||||||||||||||||||||||||||||||||||||||||||||||||||||||||||||||||||||||

Makes 4 servings

Shrimp shooters are a fun way to kick off happy hour. Seasoned shrimp smothered in a spicy cocktail sauce offers two levels of flavor to enjoy.

|||||||||||||||||||||||||||||||||||||||||

Variation

For a smoother sauce, place the Mexican Cocktail Sauce in Step 1 in a blender or food processor and pulse until smooth, 1 to 2 minutes.

- 4 martini glasses or 4 oversize shot glasses
- Baking sheet, lined with foil

Mexican Cocktail Sauce

1 cup	Tomato Table Salsa (page 57) or store-bought	250 mL
1 tbsp	prepared horseradish	15 mL
	Juice of 2 limes	
	Freshly ground black pepper	
3	cloves garlic, minced	3
½ cup	olive oil	125 mL
	Juice of 2 limes	
1 tbsp	minced cilantro	15 mL
16	jumbo raw shrimp, peeled and deveined	16
	Kosher salt	
1 cup	shredded cabbage	250 mL
	Tequila	
1	lime, cut into 4 wedges	1

1. *Mexican Cocktail Sauce:* In a small bowl, combine salsa, horseradish and lime juice. Season with pepper to taste. Cover and refrigerate until ready to serve, for up to 2 hours.

2. In a small resealable container, combine garlic, olive oil, lime juice and cilantro. Add shrimp and toss to combine. Cover and refrigerate for at least 30 minutes or for up to 1 hour.

3. Preheat broiler with rack 3 to 5 inches (7.5 to 12.5 cm) from heat.

4. Remove shrimp from marinade, discarding marinade. Place shrimp on prepared baking sheet. Lightly season with salt. Broil shrimp, turning once, for 3 to 4 minutes per side until opaque and slightly charred. Let cool completely.

5. Divide cabbage equally among martini glasses. Arrange 4 shrimp in each glass. Top with equal amounts of Mexican Cocktail Sauce. Garnish with a splash of tequila and wedge of lime.

Stuffed Jalapeños

This is a relatively new appetizer that has become a favorite among Mexican food lovers. There are many ways to stuff jalapeños. Some versions are deep-fried but I like this fresher, lighter version. Additionally, the simplicity of wrapping a stuffed chile to create a tempting appetizer is addictive. So try the Bacon Jalapeño variation as well.

Tips

I have gotten the best results by using a broiler pan or a small rack inserted in a jelly-roll pan. This enables the heat to rotate around the peppers and allow the juices to drain off. It keeps the peppers from getting soggy on the bottom.

Jalapeños can create a heat sensation on your skin. Kitchen gloves help protect your hands.

To make ahead, follow Steps 1 and 2. Place in an airtight container and refrigerate overnight or freeze for up to 3 months. Thaw at room temperature and continue with Step 3.

- Preheat oven to 425°F (220°C)
- Broiler pan, greased (see Tips, left)

12	medium jalapeño peppers (see Tips, left)	12
8 oz	cream cheese	250 g
½ cup	shredded Monterey Jack cheese	125 mL

1. Slice each jalapeño in half lengthwise. Using a spoon, scoop out seeds and ribs from jalapeño, leaving stems intact. You will have 24 halves.

2. In a medium bowl, combine cream cheese and cheese. Mix well. Place about 1 tbsp (15 mL) of filling into each jalapeño half. Place on prepared broiling pan.

3. Bake in preheated oven until peppers are soft and filling is bubbly, 25 to 30 minutes.

Variations

Add 1 tbsp (15 mL) minced green onion, green parts only, and ¼ tsp (1 mL) ground cumin to cream cheese in Step 2.

Bacon Jalapeños: Follow Steps 1 and 2. Cut 8 slices of bacon into 3 equal pieces. Place one slice on top of each jalapeño. Continue with Step 3. Bake in preheated oven until peppers are soft, filling is bubbling and bacon is crispy, 30 to 35 minutes.

Bacon and Green Chile Quesadillas

| Makes 6 wedges |

A quesadilla is a toasted flour tortilla filled with melted cheese and yummy ingredients. Bacon and chile are a delightful combination.

Tip

I enjoy using Mexican cheeses in my quesadillas. Here are a few suggestions: Asadero, Queso Blanco, Queso Quesadilla and Manchego cheeses are among many cheeses that melt easily and are used in quesadillas and many Mexican recipes due to their creamy and rich elements. Asadero cheese has a smooth texture, is yellow in color and has a tangy yet mild flavor. Queso Blanco and Queso Quesadilla cheeses are mild in flavor and white in color. Manchego is a buttery yellow cheese with a salty, nutty flavor.

1 tsp	olive oil, divided	5 mL
2	10- to 12-inch (25 to 30 cm) flour tortillas	2
1½ cups	shredded Monterey Jack cheese or Cheddar cheese (see Tip, left)	375 mL
4	slices bacon, cooked and finely chopped	4
¼ cup	roasted green chile peppers (see page 98)	60 mL
	Classic Guacamole (page 51) or store-bought	
	Roasted Tomato Salsa (page 56) or store-bought	

1. In a large skillet, heat ½ tsp (2 mL) of the oil over medium-high heat. Brush to coat pan evenly with oil. Place one tortilla in the skillet and cook until air bubbles begin to form, about 1 minute. Flip over and spread half of the cheese evenly over the tortilla, covering to the edges (do not let tortilla get crispy).

2. Reduce heat to medium and, working quickly, arrange half each of the bacon and green chiles over the cheese. Cook until the cheese starts to melt, about 1 minute, then fold tortilla in half to create a half-moon shape. Flip folded tortilla over and cook until tortilla is lightly toasted and cheese filling is completely melted, 1 to 2 minutes. Transfer quesadilla to a cutting board. Add remaining oil to skillet and repeat with second tortilla, cheese, bacon and green chiles.

3. Cut each quesadilla into 3 wedges and serve hot with guacamole and salsa.

Veggie Quesadillas

Makes 6 wedges

I love the combination of fresh vegetables nestled in warm melted cheese. This quesadilla is addictive. Switch up the vegetables depending on what you have on hand. They are light, fresh and delicious.

Tip

You can use cooking spray instead of the olive oil.

1 tsp	olive oil, divided (see Tip, left)	5 mL
2	10- to 12-inch (25 to 30 cm) flour tortillas	2
1½ cups	shredded Monterey Jack cheese or Cheddar cheese (see Tip, page 39)	375 mL
2 tbsp	diced red onion	30 mL
2 tbsp	diced red or green bell pepper	30 mL
4	mushrooms, diced	4
½ cup	tomato, seeded and diced	125 mL
	Classic Guacamole (page 51) or store-bought	
	Salsa Verde (page 58) or store-bought	

1. In a large skillet, heat ½ tsp (2 mL) of the oil over medium-high heat. Brush to coat pan evenly with oil. Place one tortilla in the skillet and cook until air bubbles begin to form, about 1 minute. Flip over and spread half of the cheese evenly over the tortilla, covering to the edges (do not let tortilla get crispy).

2. Reduce the heat to medium and, working quickly, arrange half each of the onion, bell pepper, mushrooms and tomato evenly over the cheese. Cook until cheese starts to melt, about 1 minute, then fold tortilla in half to create a half-moon shape. Flip folded tortilla over and cook until tortilla is lightly toasted and cheese filling is completely melted, 1 to 2 minutes. Transfer quesadilla to a cutting board. Add remaining oil to skillet and repeat with the second tortilla, cheese and vegetables.

3. Cut each quesadilla into 3 wedges. Serve hot with guacamole and salsa verde.

Variations

Other vegetables work well in quesadillas. Try 2 tbsp (30 mL) chopped black olives, 2 chopped artichoke hearts, and 2 chopped green onions, whites and greens.

Sautéed vegetables add a different texture to these quesadillas. In a skillet over medium heat, heat 1 tsp (5 mL) olive oil. Add onion, bell pepper, mushrooms and tomato and cook, stirring, until soft, 3 to 4 minutes. Set aside. Arrange vegetable mixture on top of cheese as directed in Step 2.

Shrimp Quesadillas

Makes 6 wedges

This is a tasty appetizer I often serve with a nice white wine. Lightly seasoned shrimp adds so much flavor to this quesadilla.

4 tsp	olive oil, divided	20 mL
10	medium cooked shrimp, chopped	10
1	clove garlic, minced	1
1	jalapeño pepper, seeded and chopped	1
	Juice of 1 lime	
2	10- to 12-inch (25 to 30 cm) flour tortillas	2
1½ cups	shredded Monterey Jack cheese or Cheddar cheese (see Tip, page 39)	375 mL
	Fiesta Guacamole (page 51) or store-bought	
	Tomatillo Avocado Salsa (page 60)	

1. In a large skillet, heat 1 tbsp (15 mL) of the oil over medium heat. Add shrimp, garlic, jalapeño and lime juice and cook, stirring, until jalapeño is soft and shrimp are heated through, 4 to 6 minutes. Transfer to a bowl and keep warm.

2. Wipe out skillet and return to medium-high heat. Add ½ tsp (2 mL) of the remaining oil and brush to coat pan evenly. Place one tortilla in the skillet and cook until air bubbles begin to form, about 1 minute. Flip over and spread half of the cheese evenly over the tortilla, covering to the edges (do not let tortilla get crispy).

3. Reduce the heat to medium and, working quickly, arrange half of the shrimp mixture evenly over cheese. Cook until cheese starts to melt, about 1 minute, then fold tortilla in half to create a half-moon shape. Flip folded tortilla over and cook until tortilla is lightly toasted and cheese filling is completely melted, 1 to 2 minutes. Transfer quesadilla to a cutting board. Add remaining oil to skillet and repeat with the second tortilla and remaining cheese and shrimp mixture.

4. Cut each quesadilla into 3 wedges and serve hot with guacamole and salsa.

Grilled Beef Quesadillas

Makes 6 wedges

The charred flavor of grilled skirt steak adds texture and flavor to this quesadilla. Perfectly garnished with pico de gallo and guacamole, this quesadilla is a crowd-pleaser.

- Preheat greased barbecue grill to medium-high (see Tip, page 43)
- Instant-read thermometer

8 oz	beef skirt steak	250 g
	Juice of 1 lime	
½ tsp	seasoned salt	2 mL
1 tsp	olive oil, divided	5 mL
2	10- to 12-inch (25 to 30 cm) flour tortillas	2
1½ cups	shredded Monterey Jack cheese or Cheddar cheese	375 mL
	Classic Guacamole (page 51) or store-bought	
	Pico de Gallo (page 56)	

1. In a glass dish, coat steak with lime juice and season with salt on both sides. Place in the refrigerator and marinate for 30 minutes or for up to 2 hours.

2. Place on preheated grill, and cook, turning once, until an instant-read thermometer registers 145°F (63°C) for medium-rare, 5 to 8 minutes per side. Transfer steak to cutting board, tent with foil and let stand for 5 minutes. Cut into bite-size pieces.

3. In a large skillet, heat ½ tsp (2 mL) of the oil over medium-high heat. Brush to coat pan evenly with oil. Place one tortilla in the skillet and cook until air bubbles begin to form, about 1 minute. Flip over and spread half of the cheese evenly over the tortilla covering to the edges (do not let tortilla get crispy).

4. Reduce the heat to medium and, working quickly, arrange half of the steak evenly over cheese. Cook until cheese starts to melt, about 1 minute, then fold tortilla in half to create a half-moon shape. Flip folded tortilla over and cook until tortilla is lightly toasted and cheese filling is completely melted, 1 to 2 minutes. Transfer quesadilla to a cutting board. Add remaining oil in skillet and repeat with the second tortilla and remaining cheese and beef.

5. Cut each quesadilla into 3 wedges and serve hot with guacamole and salsa.

Grilled Chicken Quesadillas

Makes 6 wedges

Char-grilled chicken and roasted green chile wrapped up in a blanket of cheese is scrumptious. This quesadilla is perfect for an appetizer but I also make it for a light dinner entrée.

Tip

For best results in grilling, brush the grill grate with vegetable oil or coat with a nonstick cooking spray before preheating the grill.

• Preheat greased barbecue grill to medium-high (see Tip, left)

1	boneless skinless chicken breast (5 to 7 oz/150 to 210 g)	1
2 tsp	olive oil, divided	10 mL
½ tsp	seasoned salt	2 mL
2	10- to 12-inch (25 to 30 mL) flour tortillas	2
1½ cups	shredded Monterey Jack cheese or Cheddar cheese	375 mL
2 tbsp	roasted green chile peppers (see page 98)	30 mL
	Charred Corn Guacamole (page 52) or store-bought	
	Salsa Verde (page 58) or store-bought	

1. Coat chicken with 1 tsp (5 mL) of the oil. Season with salt on both sides.

2. Place on preheated grill and cook, turning once, until no longer pink inside, 6 to 8 minutes per side. Transfer to a cutting board, tent with foil and let stand for 6 to 8 minutes. Cut into bite-size pieces.

3. In a large skillet, heat ½ tsp (2 mL) of the oil over medium-high heat. Brush to coat pan evenly with oil. Place one tortilla in the skillet and cook until air bubbles begin to form, about 1 minute. Flip over and spread half of the cheese evenly over the tortilla, covering to the edges (do not let tortilla get crispy).

4. Reduce the heat to medium and, working quickly, arrange half each of the chicken and chiles evenly over the cheese. Cook until cheese starts to melt about 1 minute, then fold tortilla in half to create a half-moon shape. Flip folded tortilla over and cook until tortilla is lightly toasted and cheese filling is completely melted, 1 to 2 minutes. Transfer quesadilla to a cutting board. Add remaining oil to skillet and repeat with the second tortilla and remaining cheese, chicken and chiles.

5. Cut each quesadilla into 3 wedges and serve hot with guacamole and salsa.

Authentic Mexican Nachos

Makes 12 nachos

It is said that the nacho was created late one summer afternoon by a Mexican restaurateur named Ignacio, "Nacho" to his friends. Whatever the circumstance, people around the globe cannot get enough of this wonderful appetizer. Simple flavors of rich cheese and pickled jalapeños create the perfect nacho. These little individual nachos are quick to make and fun to eat.

- Preheat broiler with rack positioned 5 inches (12.5 cm) from the heat
- Ovenproof platter

12	round or triangle crispy corn tortilla chips, about 2 inches (5 cm)	12
3/4 cup	shredded Cheddar cheese	175 mL
12	pickled jalapeño pepper slices, drained	12

1. Arrange chips close together but not touching on ovenproof platter. Top each chip equally with cheese. Place 1 slice of jalapeño on top of each chip.

2. Broil until cheese is melted and bubbly, 1 to 2 minutes. Watch carefully so nachos do not burn!

Variations

For more flavor, top each chip with 1 tsp (5 mL) of refried beans before adding cheese.

After broiling and just before serving, top each nacho with 1 tsp (5 mL) Fiery Corn Salsa (page 59) or Pico de Gallo (page 56).

Nachos Grande

Makes 6 servings

Piled high with flavor, this variation of the nacho is served in many eateries throughout the Southwest. This plate of goodness — crispy chips layered with melted cheese — is garnished with fresh tomato and olives.

Tip

If you are pressed for time, substitute canned refried beans.

- Preheat broiler with rack positioned 8 inches (20 cm) from the heat
- Ovenproof platter

36	Fresh Tortilla Chips (corn) (page 34)	36
1¼ cups	Stove Top Refried Beans (page 100) or store-bought	300 mL
1½ cups	shredded Cheddar Cheese	375 mL
⅓ cup	pickled jalapeño pepper slices, drained	75 mL
⅓ cup	Classic Guacamole (page 51) or store-bought	75 mL
¼ cup	sour cream	60 mL
½ cup	sliced black olives	125 mL
1	tomato, seeded and diced	1

1. Lay 18 chips on an ovenproof platter. Lightly spread chips with half of the beans, leaving some uncovered. Sprinkle half of the cheese evenly over all the chips. Top with half of the jalapeño slices. Repeat to make a second layer with remaining chips, beans, cheese and jalapeños. Broil until cheese is melted and bubbly throughout, 6 to 8 minutes.

2. Garnish with guacamole and sour cream in the center of the nachos. Top with olives and tomato.

> ## Variation
>
> For beefy nachos, add 12 oz (375 g) cooked ground beef, seasoned with salt and pepper to taste before adding cheese on each layer.

Carne Asada Nachos

Makes 36 nachos	

The tangy flavor of Carne Asada make this appetizer a meal in itself and so irresistible.

- Preheat broiler with rack positioned 8 inches (20 cm) from heat
- Ovenproof platter

36	Fresh Tortilla Chips (corn) (page 34)	36
1½ cups	shredded Cheddar cheese or Monterey Jack cheese	375 mL
⅓ cup	pickled jalapeño pepper slices, drained	75 mL
2 cups	Carne Asada (page 164), cut into bite-size pieces	500 mL
	Fiesta Guacamole (page 51) or store-bought	
⅓ cup	sour cream	75 mL
½ cup	sliced black olives	125 mL
1	tomato, seeded and diced	1

1. Place half of the chips side by side on ovenproof platter. Sprinkle half of the cheese evenly over chips. Top with half of the jalapeño slices and half of the Carne Asada. Repeat to make a second layer. Broil until cheese is melted and bubbly throughout, 6 to 8 minutes.

2. Garnish with guacamole and sour cream in the center of the nachos. Top with olives and tomato.

Variations

For Chicken Nachos: Substitute 2 cups (500 mL) Pollo Asada (see Variation, page 164) for Carne Asada in Step 1.

Substitute 2 fresh jalapeño peppers, seeded and thinly sliced into rings, for pickled jalapeños.

Garden Nachos

||||||||||||||||||||||||||||||||||||||||||||||||||||||||||||||||||||||||||||||||||||||||

Makes 6 servings

I like warm crispy chips and melted cheese with fresh vegetable flavors. This nacho offers just that right balance in texture and taste.

||||||||||||||||||||||||||||||||||||||||||

- Preheat broiler with rack positioned 5 inches (12.5 cm) from heat
- Ovenproof platter

2 tbsp	minced cilantro	30 mL
1	tomato, seeded and diced	1
2	green onions, greens parts only, diced	2
12	round or triangle crispy corn tortilla chips, about 2 inches (5 cm)	12
¾ cup	shredded Cheddar cheese or Monterey Jack cheese	175 mL
¼ cup	roasted green chile peppers (see page 98)	60 mL

1. In a small bowl, combine cilantro, tomato and green onions. Set aside.

2. Arrange chips close together on ovenproof platter. Top each chip equally with cheese. Place chiles equally on top of each chip. Broil until cheese is melted and bubbling, 1 to 2 minutes. Watch carefully so nachos do not burn!

3. Sprinkle with cilantro mixture.

Variation

For additional fresh flavor, serve with Pico de Gallo (page 56) or Fiery Corn Salsa (page 59) on the side.

Tostaditos

Makes 12 tostaditos

These little tostadas are great for kicking off a celebration. Light and tasty bites of crispy corn tortilla chips, refried beans and fresh garnish all in a bite or two!

12	round crispy corn tortilla chips, about 2 inches (5 cm)	12
¾ cup	Stove Top Refried Beans, warmed (page 100) or store-bought	175 mL
¾ cup	shredded lettuce	175 mL
½ cup	shredded Cheddar or Monterey Jack cheese	125 mL
	Fiesta Taco Sauce (page 66)	

1. Spread a thin layer of beans on each chip. Place on a platter. Top each chip with equal amounts of lettuce and cheese. Drizzle with taco sauce.

Variation

Chicken Tostaditos: Coat 1 boneless skinless chicken breast (5 to 7 oz/150 to 210 g) with oil and season with seasoned salt. Preheated greased barbecue grill to medium-high. Grill chicken, turning once, until no longer pink inside, 6 to 8 minutes per side. Transfer chicken to a cutting board, tent with foil and let stand for 6 to 8 minutes. Chop chicken into small pieces. After beans are spread on chips divide chicken equally among chips. Top each chip with equal amounts of lettuce and cheese. Drizzle with taco sauce.

Ceviche

Makes 2 cups		
(500 mL)		

I love ceviche — citrus marinated fish tossed with fresh chiles, tomatoes and spices. Flavor is added by marinating the fish in a citrus bath. The citric acid of the lime naturally poaches the fish without heat.

Tip

There are concerns about the sustainability of some fish and seafood so we recommend you check reliable sites such as www.seachoice.org for the latest information.

1 lb	halibut steak (see Tip, left)	500 g
	Juice of 10 limes	
1	onion, finely chopped	1
5	tomatoes, seeded and finely chopped	5
2	jalapeño peppers, seeded and minced	2
1	yellow chile pepper, seeded and minced	1
1	clove garlic, minced	1
	Kosher salt and freshly ground black pepper	
1 tbsp	minced cilantro	15 mL
	Fresh Tortilla Chips, warmed (corn) (page 34)	

1. Rinse halibut and pat dry with paper towel. Cut into $\frac{1}{4}$-inch (0.5 cm) cubes. In a large bowl, combine fish and lime juice. Add onion, tomatoes, jalapeños, chile pepper and garlic. Cover and refrigerate, stirring occasionally, for 2 hours or for up to 4 hours.

2. Just before serving season with salt and pepper and add cilantro. Serve with tortilla chips.

Variation

You can use other firm flesh fish such as red snapper fillets, catfish or tilapia.

Shrimp Ceviche

|||||||||||||||||||||||||||||||||||||||||||||||||||||||||||||||||||||||||||||||||||

Makes 3 cups (750 mL)

This recipe is like a seafood salsa in which citrus and chile complement each other. The citrus adds a hint of sweetness to this ceviche.

|||||||||||||||||||||||||||||||||||||||||||||

Tip

I blanch the shrimp in this recipe. Unlike raw fish, shellfish needs to be cooked just a bit to eliminate any bacteria.

1 lb	medium shrimp, peeled and deveined (see Tip, left)	500 g
	Ice water	
	Juice of 4 limes	
	Juice of 2 oranges	
1	jalapeño pepper, seeded and minced	1
1	yellow chile pepper, seeded and minced	1
½ cup	minced red onion	125 mL
½ cup	chopped celery	125 mL
½ cup	chopped peeled cucumber	125 mL
1 tbsp	minced cilantro	15 mL
	Kosher salt and freshly ground black pepper	
	Fresh Tortilla Chips, warmed (corn) (page 34)	

1. In a large pot of boiling water, cook shrimp until opaque and pink, about 2 minutes. Drain immediately and transfer to a bowl of ice water to cool. Drain and transfer to a cutting board. Chop into bite-size pieces.

2. In a large bowl, combine lime and orange juices. Add jalapeño, yellow pepper, red onion, celery and cucumber. Add shrimp and mix well. Cover and refrigerate, stirring occasionally, for 2 hours or for up to 4 hours.

3. Just before serving, garnish with cilantro and season with salt and pepper. Serve with tortilla chips.

Classic Guacamole

Makes 2 cups (500 mL)

This is a classic version of guacamole that is tasty and simple with onion, garlic, lime and seasonings. I serve it in tacos, on tortas and offer it with chips and salsa.

Tip

You can mash up avocado into a creamy consistency or mash some and dice the rest of the avocado for a semi-creamy/chunky-style guacamole.

6	avocados, mashed	6
1	clove garlic, minced	1
¼ cup	minced onion	60 mL
2 tbsp	freshly squeezed lime juice	30 mL
	Kosher or sea salt	

1. In a large bowl, gently combine avocados, garlic and onion. Add lime juice and mix well. Add salt to taste. Serve immediately or transfer to an airtight container and refrigerate, stirring occasionally, for 30 minutes or for up to 2 hours.

Fiesta Guacamole

Makes 3 cups (750 mL)

A good guacamole has to have balance in flavor. The avocados, fresh vegetables and chile blend well with the flavors of the citrusy juices.

Variation

When I am pressed for time I omit the tomato, onion and green onions and add ½ cup (125 mL) tomato-based salsa instead.

6	avocados, mashed	6
1	tomato, seeded and chopped	1
¼ cup	minced onion	60 mL
1	jalapeño pepper, diced	1
2	green onions, green parts only, chopped	2
2 tbsp	freshly squeezed lime juice	30 mL
	Kosher or sea salt	

1. In a large bowl, gently combine avocados, tomato, onion, jalapeño and green onions. Add lime juice and mix well. Add salt to taste. Serve immediately or transfer to an airtight container and refrigerate, stirring occasionally, for 30 minutes or for up to 2 hours.

Variation

Add 1 tbsp (15 mL) minced cilantro.

Charred Corn Guacamole

Make 2 cups (500 mL)

This is a kicked up version of guacamole. The roasted corn adds a nice flavor and texture.

Tip

You can use canned corn, drained; frozen corn, thawed; or cooked corn cut from the cob. For an added smoky flavor, use corn grilled on the barbecue grill.

- Preheat broiler with rack positioned 5 inches (12.5 cm) from heat
- Ovenproof platter

½ cup	roasted green chile peppers (see page 98)	125 mL
1 cup	corn kernels (see Tip, left)	250 mL
1 tbsp	freshly squeezed lime juice	15 mL
2 tsp	olive oil	10 mL
¼ tsp	ground cumin	1 mL
4	avocados	4
	Seasoned salt	

1. In a medium bowl, combine chile, corn, lime juice, oil and cumin. Transfer to a baking sheet and broil until corn is slightly charred, 3 to 4 minutes. Remove and let cool completely.

2. In a large bowl, slightly mash avocados. Add corn mixture and stir gently to combine. Add salt to taste. Serve immediately or transfer to an airtight container and refrigerate, stirring occasionally, for 30 minutes or for up to 2 hours.

Chile con Queso

||||||||||||||||||||||||||||||||||||||||||||||||||||||||||||||||||||||||||||||||||||||||||||||||||||||||

Makes 3¹/₂ cups (875 mL)

A balance of good texture and taste is the foundation for the perfect queso. It has to be smooth and creamy yet thick enough to cling to a taco or chip. This combination of cheeses ensures a good consistency and blends fresh chile and tomato flavors throughout.

Tip

To make ahead, transfer to an airtight container and refrigerate for up to 4 days. To reheat, place in a microwave-safe bowl and microwave on Medium for 30 seconds. Repeat until queso is completely melted.

2 cups	shredded Cheddar cheese	500 mL
1 cup	shredded Monterey Jack cheese	250 mL
1½ tsp	cornstarch	7 mL
¾ cup	chicken broth	175 mL
¾ cup	roasted green chile peppers (see page 98)	175 mL
1	tomato, seeded and diced	1
12 oz	pasteurized prepared cheese product, such as Velveeta, cut into cubes	375 g

1. In a large bowl, combine Cheddar and Monterey Jack cheeses with cornstarch. Mix well until cheese is well coated.

2. In a large pot, heat broth over medium-high heat. Add chiles and tomato and cook, stirring, until tomato is soft, 4 to 6 minutes. Reduce heat to medium-low and stir in shredded cheese mixture. Add processed cheese, a few cubes at a time, stirring until smooth. Serve immediately or let cool completely at room temperature

Variation

If using a slow cooker, follow Step 1. In Step 2, after adding shredded cheese mixture, transfer to a slow cooker set on Low. Add processed cheese, stirring until smooth. Cook, stirring occasionally, for up to 2 hours.

Queso con Chorizo

Makes 4 servings

This queso is popular in the northern parts of Mexico. It is also known as Queso Fundido, a creamy white cheese laced with Mexican sausage and chile.

Tip

You can substitute Cheddar cheese for the white American cheese. It will keep the flavor but just slightly change the color.

- Preheat oven to 350°F (180°C)
- Ovenproof dish or 8-inch (20 cm) square baking dish

1 cup	shredded mozzarella or Asadero cheese	250 mL
1 cup	shredded Monterey Jack cheese	250 mL
1 cup	shredded white American cheese (see Tip, left)	250 mL
4 oz	cooked fresh chorizo sausage, drained and crumbled	125 g
1/3 cup	roasted green chile peppers (see page 98)	75 mL
1/4 cup	half-and-half (10%) cream	60 mL
	Fresh Tortilla Chips, warmed (corn) (page 34)	

1. In a large bowl, combine mozzarella, Monterey Jack and American cheeses. Add chorizo and chile peppers and stir gently to combine. Drizzle with cream and mix well. Transfer to baking dish.

2. Bake in preheated oven, stirring occasionally, until cheese is melted, 10 to 14 minutes. Serve with warm corn tortilla chips.

Salsas, Relishes and Sauces

Pico de Gallo

Makes 2 cups (500 mL)

This is a salsa I use more than any other. This crisp, refreshing flavors capture the true essence of Mexico! I can't think of a Mexican dish this does not taste good on. Try it on warm, crispy tortilla chips.

4	tomatoes, seeded and diced	4
4	green onions, greens parts only, minced	4
3	jalapeño peppers, seeded and minced	3
2	serrano chile peppers, seeded and minced	2
1	onion, finely chopped	1
2 tbsp	minced fresh cilantro	30 mL
	Juice of 2 limes	
	Kosher salt	

1. In a large bowl, combine tomatoes, green onions, jalapeños, serrano chiles, onion and cilantro. Add lime juice and mix well. Transfer to an airtight container and refrigerate, stirring occasionally, for 1 hour or for up to 24 hours. Add salt to taste just before serving.

Roasted Tomato Salsa

Makes about 2 cups (500 mL)

This basic tomato salsa is delicious on just about any Mexican dish. The charred skin of the roasted tomatoes adds an earthy flavor that blends well with the roasted jalapeños. It makes a great "chip and dip" salsa.

Variation

Substitute 1 tbsp (15 mL) minced fresh cilantro for the parsley.

- Preheat broiler
- Blender

4 to 6	tomatoes, unpeeled	4 to 6
3 to 4	roasted jalapeño peppers, skin on (see page 98)	3 to 4
1	onion, chopped	1
2	green onions, green parts only, chopped	2
1 tbsp	minced Italian flat-leaf parsley	15 mL
	Salt	

1. Place tomatoes on a baking sheet and broil, turning often, until skins are charred, 3 to 4 minutes.

2. In a blender, pulse charred tomatoes, jalapeños, onion and green onions until thick and slightly chunky. Pour into an airtight container. Add salt to taste. Refrigerate, stirring occasionally, for 1 hour or for up to 2 days.

Tomato Table Salsa

Makes 3¹/₂ cups (875 mL)

I always keep a can of diced tomatoes in the pantry and hot pepper flakes in my spice rack, then just grab the fresh ingredients for this salsa on the run. I like it on fresh, crispy tortilla chips.

Tip

Hot pepper flakes give this salsa its heat. The pepper flakes often vary in heat levels, so add an additional 1 tsp (5 mL) for more heat, if desired.

1	can (28 oz/796 mL) diced tomatoes	1
¹/₂ cup	chopped roasted green chile peppers (see page 98)	125 mL
3 to 4	green onions, white parts and a bit of green, chopped	3 to 4
1	onion, finely chopped	1
2	clove garlic, minced	2
2 tsp	hot pepper flakes (see Tip, left)	10 mL
	Salt	

1. In a large bowl, combine tomatoes, chiles, green onions to taste, onion, garlic, hot pepper flakes and salt. Transfer to an airtight container and refrigerate, stirring occasionally, for 30 minutes or for up to 2 hours.

Variation

Taco-Style Sauce: Omit hot pepper flakes. Substitute 5 jalapeños, seeds removed, for the green chile. Place in a small pot and cover with water. Boil until jalapeños are soft, about 10 minutes. Place half of the jalapeños, half of the tomatoes, green onions, onion and garlic in a blender and pulse until blended. Pour into a large bowl. Repeat with remaining jalapeño, tomato, green onions, onion and garlic. Add salt to taste. Transfer to an airtight container and refrigerate, stirring occasionally, for 30 minutes or for up to 2 hours.

Green Chile and Jalapeño Salsa

Makes 2 cups (500 mL)

This is a salsa that is simmered and cooked to perfection. I like to serve it warm in the winter months. It enhances the flavor of grilled meats and poultry yet is perfect with a bowl of warm crispy corn tortilla chips.

1 tbsp	olive oil	15 mL
2	cloves garlic, minced	2
4	jalapeño peppers, seeded and minced	4
½ cup	minced onion	125 mL
1½ cups	chopped roasted green chile peppers (see page 98)	375 mL
	Kosher salt	

1. In a large skillet, heat oil over medium heat. Add garlic and cook until soft, about 1 minute. Add jalapeños and onion and cook until onion is softened, 3 to 4 minutes. Reduce heat to medium-low and add green chiles. Cook until flavors are well blended, 4 to 6 minutes. Add salt to taste. Serve immediately or let cool completely and transfer to an airtight container and refrigerate, stirring occasionally, for 1 hour or for up to 2 days.

Salsa Verde

Makes 2 cups (500 mL)

I love this salsa. Served chilled, at room temperature or even heated, it is very versatile.

Tip

Substitute pickled jalapeños for roasted jalapeños. You'll need ½ cup (125 mL) drained and chopped.

● Blender or food processor

2 cups	chopped roasted green chile peppers (see page 98), about 12	500 mL
4	roasted jalapeño peppers (see Tip, left and page 98)	4
2	cloves garlic, minced	2
1 tbsp	olive oil	15 mL
1	onion, chopped	1
	Juice of 1 lime	
	Salt	

1. In a blender, pulse green chiles, jalapeños, garlic, olive oil, onion and lime juice until slightly chunky, 1 to 2 minutes. Pour into an airtight container. Add salt to taste. Refrigerate, stirring occasionally, for 1 hour or for up to 2 days.

Citrus Salsa

**Makes 2 cups
(500 mL)**

Citrus lovers will enjoy the freshness of this salsa spiked with chile. Jicama and mango add interesting textures and great flavor to chicken and fish tacos.

Tip

Jicama is a root vegetable that adds texture. It has little flavor but takes on the flavor of the spices, herbs and juices around it.

2	oranges	2
1	lime	1
½	grapefruit	½
¼ cup	chopped jicama (see Tip, left)	60 mL
2 tsp	hot pepper flakes, divided	10 mL
1	mango, diced	1

1. Remove pith and skin from oranges, lime and grapefruit and cut into chunks.

2. In a large bowl, combine oranges, lime, grapefruit, jicama and 1 tsp (5 mL) of the hot pepper flakes. Gently add mango and toss. Transfer to an airtight container and refrigerate, stirring occasionally, for 30 minutes or for up to 2 hours. Taste for heat levels and add remaining pepper flakes before serving, if desired.

Fiery Corn Salsa

**Makes 2 cups
(500 mL)**

I like serving more than one salsa when I serve Mexican food. Refreshing sweet corn makes a crisp, crunchy salsa that will capture attention. It is fresh tasting and colorful.

Tip

You can use canned corn, drained; frozen corn, thawed; or corn from the cob, cooked on the stove top. For a smoky flavor, use corn grilled on the barbecue grill.

¼ cup	olive oil	60 mL
3 tbsp	freshly squeezed lime juice	45 mL
2 tsp	minced fresh cilantro	10 mL
3	tomatoes, seeded and diced	3
1½ cups	corn kernels (see Tip, left)	375 mL
2 to 3	jalapeño peppers, seeded and diced	2 to 3
	Salt and freshly ground black pepper	

1. In a large bowl, combine oil, lime juice and cilantro. Add tomatoes, corn and jalapeños to taste. Mix well until corn mixture is well coated. Season with salt and pepper to taste. Transfer to an airtight container and refrigerate, stirring occasionally, for 1 hour or for up to 2 days.

Tomatillo Avocado Salsa

Makes 2 cups (500 mL)

Amazingly, tomatillos have an intense citrusy flavor that blends well with the smooth, rich flavor of the avocado. I love the pungent flavor of fresh cilantro so the more the merrier for me!

Tips

Tomatillos are a small green tomato-like fruit covered in a green filmy husk. They have a citrusy flavor and are perfect for sauces and salsas. Remove the husks and wash tomatillos thoroughly to remove stickiness.

Cilantro is a green flat-leaf herb that has a distinctive pungent flavor and should be soaked and rinsed in water several times to clean before using to avoid gritty texture.

I prefer kosher or sea salt because it has a lighter, cleaner flavor.

● Blender or food processor

12	tomatillos, peeled, cored and chopped (see Tips, left)	12
6	green onions, green parts only, chopped	6
3	jalapeño peppers, seeded and chopped	3
1 to 2	cloves garlic, coarsely chopped	1 to 2
1 cup	cilantro leaves (see Tips, left)	250 mL
½ tsp	kosher salt (see Tips, left)	2 mL
2	avocados	2

1. In a blender, pulse tomatillos, green onions, jalapeños, garlic to taste, cilantro and salt until slightly chunky. Transfer to an airtight container and refrigerate, stirring occasionally, for 1 hour or for up to 2 hours. Before serving, cube avocados and gently fold in.

Variation

For a milder version, substitute 1 poblano chile pepper, seeded and chopped, for the jalapeños.

Red Onion Relish

**Makes 2 cups
(500 mL)**

This sweet-savory relish is a rendition of my dad's favorite garnish. It is tangy and fresh tasting on tacos or as a garnish for burritos, tortas or enchiladas.

1 cup	red wine vinegar	250 mL
¼ cup	vegetable oil	60 mL
¼ cup	granulated sugar	60 mL
2	red onions, diced	2

1. In a large bowl, whisk together vinegar, oil and sugar. Add red onions and toss until well coated. Transfer to an airtight container and refrigerate, stirring occasionally, for 1 hour or for up to 2 days.

Green Chile Relish

**Makes 2 cups
(500 mL)**

I have been snacking on this relish for years. I serve it on grilled steak, fish tacos and even veggie tacos. A simple pleasure is serving this relish with cocktail crackers or crispy corn tortilla chips.

2 cups	chopped roasted green chile peppers (see page 98)	500 mL
¼ cup	olive oil	60 mL
5	cloves garlic, minced	5
1 tsp	crushed Mexican oregano	5 mL
	Kosher salt	

1. In a large bowl, combine chiles, oil, garlic, oregano and salt to taste. Transfer to an airtight container and refrigerate, stirring occasionally, for 1 hour or for up to 2 days.

Garlic and Jalapeño Relish

||||||||||||||||||||||||||||||||||||||||||||||||||||||||||||||||||||||

1 tbsp	olive oil	15 mL
5	cloves garlic, minced	5
5	jalapeño peppers, seeded and minced	5
¾ cup	chopped green onion, green parts only	175 mL
	Kosher salt and freshly ground black pepper	

Makes 1 cup (250 mL)

This sautéed relish is rich in flavor. Serve it warm or at room temperature for the best flavor on grilled meats and poultry.

||||||||||||||||||||||||||||||||||||||||

1. In a large skillet, heat oil and garlic over medium heat. Add jalapeños and green onion and cook, stirring, until vegetables are tender-crisp, 6 to 8 minutes. Season with salt and pepper to taste. Serve warm or let cool to room temperature. Transfer to an airtight container and refrigerate, stirring occasionally, for 1 hour or for up to 2 days.

Cabbage Relish

||||||||||||||||||||||||||||||||||||||||||||||||||||||||||||||||||||||

3 tbsp	freshly squeezed lime juice	45 mL
2 tbsp	olive oil	30 mL
1 tsp	hot pepper flakes	5 mL
2 cups	finely shredded green cabbage	500 mL
1 cup	finely shredded red cabbage	250 mL

Makes 3 cups (750 mL)

Shredded cabbage can take on so many flavors. This relish is laced with fresh lime and chile. It can be used as a garnish on tacos, enchiladas or burritos, adding just the right amount of freshness to every entrée.

||||||||||||||||||||||||||||||||||||||||

1. In a small bowl, combine lime juice, oil and hot pepper flakes and whisk until well blended.

2. In a large bowl, combine green and red cabbage. Add dressing mixture and toss until cabbage is well coated. Transfer to an airtight container and refrigerate, stirring occasionally, for up to 2 days.

Variation

Omit the lime and hot pepper flakes and toss cabbage with 3 tbsp (45 mL) rice vinegar and salt and pepper to taste.

Red Enchilada Sauce

Makes 2 cups (500 mL)

This authentic sauce is traditional in some regions of the Southwest. Made from dried red chiles, it is a time-consuming process but worth the effort.

Tips

There are a variety of store-bought red enchilada sauces on the market. You can find them in the Mexican food section of your grocery store or online.

Dried New Mexico red chile peppers are generally 4 to 6 inches (10 to 15 cm) in length. They can be found in the produce department or Mexican food section.

• Blender or food processor

6 to 8	dried New Mexico red chile peppers (see Tips, left)	6 to 8
6 tbsp	vegetable oil, divided	90 mL
4	cloves garlic, minced	4
2 tbsp	all-purpose flour	30 mL
	Kosher salt and freshly ground black pepper	

1. Place chiles in a bowl and cover with 1 quart (1 L) of water. Refrigerate overnight. This will soften the chiles.

2. Drain soaking liquid from chiles, reserving liquid. In a blender, purée chiles with $1\frac{1}{2}$ cups (375 mL) reserved liquid until smooth. Purée should be thick but pourable. Add additional soaking liquid, if needed. Press chile purée through a fine-mesh sieve or a strainer, discarding skin and seeds.

3. In a large skillet, heat 2 tbsp (30 mL) of the oil over medium heat. Add chile purée and garlic. Bring to a gentle boil. Reduce heat to low and simmer, stirring occasionally, until flavors are well blended, 8 to 10 minutes. Set aside.

4. In a small saucepan, heat remaining $\frac{1}{4}$ cup (60 mL) of oil over medium heat. Gradually stir in flour, creating a roux (a thick paste). Remove from heat.

5. Increase heat to medium. Gradually stir roux into chile sauce. Reduce heat and simmer, stirring, until thick and smooth, 6 to 8 minutes. Season with salt and pepper to taste. Serve immediately or let cool to room temperature. Transfer to an airtight container and refrigerate for up to 2 days.

Green Enchilada Sauce

Makes 2 cups (500 mL)		

This smooth, spicy sauce highlights fresh green chile peppers. It is good for dipping and smothering enchiladas, burritos and tacos.

Tip

Add additional 1 to 2 tbsp (15 to 30 mL) chicken broth at a time for a thinner sauce.

1	tomato, seeded and diced	1
1½ cups	chopped roasted green chile peppers (see page 98)	375 mL
2	cloves garlic, minced	2
1 cup	chicken broth (see Tip, left)	250 mL
2 tbsp	olive oil	30 mL
¼ cup	all-purpose flour	60 mL
	Kosher salt and freshly ground black pepper	

1. In a large skillet, combine tomato, chiles, garlic and broth and bring to a boil over medium-high heat. Reduce heat and bring to a gentle boil. Boil until vegetables are tender, 6 to 8 minutes.

2. In a small saucepan, heat oil over medium heat. Gradually stir in flour, creating a roux (a thick paste). Remove from heat.

3. Gradually stir roux into chile sauce over medium heat, whisking until smooth and thick, 6 to 8 minutes. Season with salt and pepper to taste. Serve immediately or let cool to room temperature. Transfer to an airtight container and refrigerate for up to 2 days.

Nachos Grande (page 45)

Fiery Corn Salsa (page 59) and
Fiesta Guacamole (page 51)

Chicken and Lime Soup (page 85)

Creamy Corn, Chile and Squash (page 96)

Chopped Mexican Salad (page 108)

Classic Rolled Tacos
(page 116)

Grilled Carne Asada Tacos (page 125)

Fresh Baja Fish Tacos (page 132)
with Basic Taco Cream Sauce (page 67)

Sonoran Enchilada Sauce

**Makes 2 cups
(500 mL)**

This is a simple sauce I serve on a variety of Mexican dishes. It is light yet has a nice spicy flavor. It is a Sonoran-style sauce served over burritos and chile rellenos.

Tip

Add additional 1 to 2 tbsp (15 to 30 mL) chicken broth at a time for a thinner sauce.

1½ tbsp	olive oil	22 mL
3	cloves garlic, minced	3
1	tomato, diced	1
½ cup	diced onion	125 mL
2 tbsp	all-purpose flour	30 mL
1½ cups	chicken broth, divided (see Tip, left)	375 mL
¼ cup	chopped roasted green chile peppers (see page 98)	60 mL
1 tbsp	minced cilantro	15 mL

1. In a large skillet, heat oil over medium-low heat. Add garlic, tomato and onion and cook, stirring, until onions are soft, 8 to 10 minutes. Reduce heat to low and add flour and stir, coating onion and tomato well, and cook for 1 minute more.

2. Slowly add chicken broth and green chiles, stirring as sauce thickens, 4 to 6 minutes. Add cilantro and cook for 2 minutes more. Set aside and let cool completely. Serve immediately or refrigerate for up to 2 days or freeze up to 3 months.

Fiesta Taco Sauce

Makes 3½ cups
(875 mL)

I love to drench my rolled tacos in this spicy tomato sauce. It is a unique balance of flavors, accented with Mexican oregano. Hot pepper flakes add heat while the onion adds texture and taste.

Tips

Mexican oregano is dried but sometimes it comes with big pieces that need to be crushed or minced.

This taco sauce has a thinner consistency than most. For a thicker sauce, add less water.

● Blender or food processor

1¾ cups	tomato sauce	425 mL
1	onion, chopped	1
1 tbsp	crushed Mexican oregano (see Tips, left)	15 mL
1 tbsp	minced garlic	15 mL
1	can (28 oz/796 mL) crushed or diced tomatoes	1
2 tbsp	hot pepper flakes	30 mL
1 tbsp	kosher salt	15 mL

1. In a large bowl, combine tomato sauce, onion, oregano, garlic and tomatoes. Add hot pepper flakes and salt.

2. In a blender, in batches, pulse tomato mixture until smooth. Pour into a large bowl and add up to 1½ cups (375 mL) of water depending on the consistency you desire (see Tips, left). Mix well. Repeat until all tomato mixture has been blended with water. Transfer sauce to a large airtight container. Cover and refrigerate, stirring occasionally, for 1 hour or for up to 4 days.

Basic Taco Cream Sauce

**Makes 1 1/4 cups
(300 mL)**

This is a basic tasty cream sauce typically served on fish tacos. I like to drizzle it on top of my chicken and fish tacos. Add the spices that you prefer to customize it for your taste (see Variations, right).

3/4 cup	mayonnaise	175 mL
1/2 cup	plain yogurt	125 mL
	Juice of 1 lime	

1. In a medium bowl, combine mayonnaise and yogurt. Add lime juice and whisk until smooth. Transfer to an airtight container or squeeze bottle. Refrigerate, stirring occasionally, for 1 hour or for up to 4 days.

Variations

Add any of the following to create a variety of different sauces: 2 garlic cloves, minced; 1 tsp (5 mL) chile powder, such as ancho or chipotle; or 1/2 tsp (2 mL) each cumin, hot pepper flakes or fresh cilantro. Season with salt to taste.

Quick Mole Sauce

Makes 2 cups (500 mL)		

There are a lot of variations of mole sauce throughout Mexico. My version is savory-sweet and easy to make. Enjoy it on grilled meats and chicken, burritos and enchiladas.

Tips

Add a pinch of cinnamon and ½ tsp (2 mL) granulated sugar for a sweeter version.

When serving this sauce, top with toasted sesame seeds.

2 cups	Red Enchilada Sauce (page 63) or store-bought	500 mL
1 tsp	hot pepper flakes	5 mL
1 tsp	dried oregano	5 mL
1 tsp	ground cumin	5 mL
1 tsp	garlic powder	5 mL
1 tsp	onion powder	5 mL
1½ oz	semisweet chocolate, chopped into small pieces	45 g

1. In a saucepan, heat sauce over medium heat. Add hot pepper flakes, oregano, cumin, garlic powder and onion powder, stirring, until well blended, 3 to 5 minutes. Reduce heat to low and add chocolate. Stir until chocolate is melted. Remove from heat.

Tortillas and Breads

Basic Corn Tortillas

Masa harina is a finely ground corn flour made from corn that is dried, cooked in water and treated with calcium hydroxide or lime. Then it is ground and dried again. By mixing it with water, it forms a dough called "masa," which is what we use to make corn tortillas.

Tip

Fresh corn tortillas do not stay fresh. They need to be used within hours of making them.

- 17 sheets wax paper, cut into 10-inch (25 cm) squares
- Tortilla press

2 cups	masa harina	500 mL
1¼ cups	very warm (almost hot) water	300 mL

1. In a large bowl, mix together masa marina and water. Knead with your hands to form the masa or dough.

2. Pinch off a golf ball size piece of masa and roll into a smooth ball. As you make each one, place balls in an airtight container until ready to use for up to 1 hour. Continue with remaining masa to make 16 balls.

3. To press tortillas, place a piece of wax paper in tortilla press and place masa ball on top. Place another piece of wax paper on top of masa ball and press to a 6-inch (15 cm) circle. Continue with remaining masa balls, stacking uncooked tortillas on a platter with wax paper sheets in between each one.

4. Heat a dry nonstick or cast-iron skillet over medium heat. Remove wax paper and transfer tortillas to skillet, one at a time, and cook, turning once, for about 45 seconds per side or until bubbly and lightly browned. Transfer tortillas to a towel-lined platter. Wrap in towel to keep warm.

Simple Corn Tortillas

Makes 16 tortillas

Tortillas with a hint of salt are perfectly balanced with the flavor of the corn. The soda adds an extra light texture to these tortillas.

Tip

Fresh corn tortillas do not stay fresh. They need to be used within hours of making them.

- 17 sheets wax paper, cut into 10-inch (25 cm) squares
- Tortilla press

2 cups	masa harina	500 mL
½ tsp	salt	2 mL
¼ tsp	baking soda	1 mL
1½ cups	very warm (almost hot) water	375 mL

1. In a large bowl, mix together masa harina, salt, baking soda and water. Knead with your hands to form the masa or dough.

2. Pinch off a golf ball size piece of masa and roll into a smooth ball. As you make each one, place balls in an airtight container until ready to use for up to 1 hour. Continue with remaining masa to make 16 balls.

3. To press tortillas, place a piece of wax paper in tortilla press and place masa ball on top. Place another piece of wax paper on top of masa ball and press to a 6-inch (15 cm) circle. Continue with remaining masa balls, stacking uncooked tortillas on a platter with wax paper sheets in between each one.

4. Heat a dry nonstick or cast-iron skillet over medium heat. Remove wax paper and transfer tortillas to skillet, one at a time, and cook, turning once, for about 45 seconds per side or until bubbly and lightly browned. Transfer tortillas to a towel-lined platter. Wrap in towel to keep warm.

Authentic Flour Tortillas

Makes 12 tortillas

Authentic Mexican tortillas are made with lard. I know some people object to using lard but it adds flavor and it really isn't all that bad for you in moderation. It has less cholesterol and saturated fat than an equal amount of butter by weight! It is the secret ingredient that makes these tortillas delicious.

Tips

Substitute ¼ cup (60 mL) vegetable oil for the lard.

Refrigerate uncooked tortillas with wax paper between layers in an airtight container for up to 8 hours. Otherwise, the dough starts to dry out.

Cooked tortillas can be stored in an airtight container and kept in the refrigerator for up to 3 days or frozen for up to 3 months.

- 13 sheets wax paper, cut into 10-inch (25 cm) squares

3 cups	all-purpose flour (approx.)	750 mL
1 tbsp	salt	15 mL
½ cup	lard (see Tips, left)	125 mL
1¼ cups	very warm (almost hot) water	300 mL

1. In a large bowl, combine flour and salt. Using your fingers, slowly work lard into flour. Add small amounts of water and continue to work with hands until dough is smooth. Form a large ball. Turn out onto a floured surface. Knead the dough thoroughly.

2. Divide dough into 12 small balls. Sprinkle each with flour and place in an airtight container. Cover and let dough stand for at least 15 minutes or for up to 1 hour.

3. On a lightly floured work surface, using a rolling pin, roll each ball out to an 8-inch (20 cm) circle. (The trick here is to turn your dough one-quarter turn each time you roll it. That will ensure you get a round tortilla.) Transfer to a wax paper square. Repeat with each dough ball and stack uncooked tortillas on a platter.

4. Heat a dry nonstick or cast-iron skillet over medium heat. Peel off wax paper from tortillas, one at a time, and cook tortillas, turning once, for about 45 seconds per side or until bubbly and lightly browned. Transfer tortillas to a towel-lined platter. Wrap in towel to keep warm.

Homemade Flour Tortillas

Makes 12 tortillas

This is a favorite from the borderland among my circle of friends. These small tortillas are perfect for my tacos, burritos and quesadillas — full of texture and flavor.

Tips

Refrigerate uncooked tortillas with wax paper between layers in an airtight container for up to 8 hours.

Cooked tortillas can be stored in an airtight container and kept in the refrigerator for up to 3 days or frozen for up to 3 months.

- 13 sheets wax paper, cut into 10-inch (25 cm) squares

4 cups	all-purpose flour (approx.)	1 L
1 tsp	salt	5 mL
1¾ cups	very warm (almost hot) water	425 mL
⅓ cup	olive oil	75 mL

1. In a large bowl, combine flour and salt. Using your fingers, slowly work water and oil into flour. Work with hands until dough is smooth. Turn out onto a floured surface and knead several times until smooth.

2. Divide dough into 12 small balls. Sprinkle each with flour and place in an airtight container. Cover and let dough stand for at least 15 minutes or for up to 1 hour.

3. On a lightly floured work surface, using a rolling pin, roll each ball out to an 8-inch (20 cm) circle. (The trick here is to turn your dough one-quarter turn each time you roll it. That will ensure you get a round tortilla.) Transfer to a wax paper square. Repeat with each dough ball and stack uncooked tortillas on a platter.

4. Heat a dry nonstick or cast-iron skillet over medium heat. Peel off wax paper from tortillas, one at a time, and cook, turning once, for about 45 seconds per side or until bubbling and lightly browned. Transfer tortillas to a towel-lined platter. Wrap in towel to keep warm.

Variation

For whole wheat tortillas, substitute 3 cups (750 mL) whole wheat flour plus 1 cup (250 mL) all-purpose flour for the 4 cups (1 L) all-purpose flour.

Reheating Tortillas

The freshest homemade tortillas make the best wraps for tacos, burritos and enchiladas. However, it is not often that I have time to make homemade tortillas and cook an entire meal in one evening. I usually make my flour and corn tortillas early in the day. Therefore, I have to reheat them before working with them in my recipes. Even the freshest store-bought tortillas need to be reheated so they are soft, pliable and easy to work with. Heating tortillas is an essential element in the success of my Mexican recipes. Corn tortillas need a bit more moisture in the reheating process than flour tortillas. Here I offer different methods for each.

Reheating Folded Taco Shells

To reheat fried taco shells or keep freshly fried shells warm, place on a baking sheet and heat in a 200°F (100°C) preheated oven for 8 to 10 minutes.

Reheating Corn and Flour Tortillas

Skillet-Warmed Corn Tortillas

This method gives you a soft, pliable tortilla that is lightly toasted on one or both sides. Place a dry nonstick or cast-iron skillet over medium heat. Place tortilla in skillet and heat each side by turning once until warm and pliable, about 1 minute per side. Place in a tortilla warmer (see page 13) or wrap in foil to keep warm until ready to use.

> **Tip**
> You can also spray each side of a corn tortilla with water for a moister consistency. For a slightly toasted texture, lightly spray one or both sides of tortilla with cooking spray before heating.

Micro-Warmed Corn or Flour Tortillas

This method gives you a very pliable and soft tortilla and allows you to roll the tacos tightly, so it's perfect for preparing rolled tacos and taquitos. It is also quick and easy for soft tacos.

Place 4 tortillas in a small plastic storage bag and close or fold over the opening. Microwave on High for 25 to 45 seconds (depending on the power of your microwave). Remove from plastic bag. The tortillas should be warm and pliable. If you leave them in too long they will be too hot to handle and will be overdone. Place in a tortilla warmer (see page 13) or wrap in foil to keep warm until ready to use.

Skillet-Warmed Flour Tortillas

In a griddle or skillet over medium-high heat, heat each tortilla on each side until soft and pliable. Place in a tortilla warmer (see page 13) or wrap in foil to keep warm until ready to use.

Oven-Warmed Flour Tortillas

Preheat oven to 275°F (140°C). Wrap 6 to 12 flour tortillas in a large piece of foil, enough to wrap around tortillas once. Seal edges tightly. Heat in preheated oven for 30 to 40 minutes.

Keeping Tortillas Warm

There are several ways to keep tortillas warm while serving. You can simply wrap fresh cooked or heated tortillas in a clean kitchen towel and place in a basket or bowl. There are also small insulated tortilla warmers with lids that are decorative.

As for large amounts of tortillas, keep them warm in an insulated chest, such as an ice chest (cooler) lined with cotton kitchen towels. Remove small amounts as needed and place in tortilla warmers.

Bolillos

Makes 12 rolls	

Fresh baked Mexican breads are a household tradition in Mexico. Bolillos accompany any Mexican meal beautifully and make a delicious torta as well.

- Stand mixer with paddle attachment
- 2 baking sheets, greased

3½ cups	all-purpose flour, divided	875 mL
1	package (¼ oz/8 g) active dry yeast	1
1 tbsp	granulated sugar	15 mL
1 tsp	salt	5 mL
1½ cups	warm water (100 to 110°F/38 to 43°C)	375 mL
	Oil	
	Cornmeal	
1	egg white	1

1. In large mixer bowl, combine 1½ cups (375 mL) of the flour, yeast, sugar and salt. Add warm water. Attach bowl to mixer and fit with paddle attachment. Beat on medium speed for 1 minute, scraping sides of bowl. Beat on high speed until dough is well blended and a bit sticky, 3 to 4 minutes. Using a wooden spoon, stir in remaining 2 cups (500 mL) of flour or enough to make a soft, not sticky dough.

2. Place dough onto a lightly floured surface. Rub a small amount of oil on hands and knead dough until it is smooth and elastic, 3 to 4 minutes.

3. Shape dough into a ball and place in a lightly greased bowl, turning once to coat. Cover and let rise in a warm, draft-free place until doubled in size, about 1 hour.

4. Punch down dough. Divide dough into 12 equal portions. Shape each portion into an oval about 4 inches (10 cm) long. Gently pull and twist each end of the oval to form points so the shape resembles a football

Tip

To make these rolls ahead, prepare and bake rolls as directed. Let cool completely. Place rolls in an airtight container or resealable freezer bag and freeze for up to 3 months. Thaw at room temperature.

5. Sprinkle cornmeal on prepared baking sheets evenly with a thin coating. Place rolls at least 3 inches (7.5 cm) apart on baking sheets. Use a sharp knife to make a cut about ¼ inch (0.5 cm) deep along center of each roll.

6. In a small bowl, whisk together egg white and ½ tsp (2 mL) water. Lightly brush each roll with egg white mixture (reserve egg white mixture). Cover and let rise until nearly double in size, 30 to 45 minutes.

7. Meanwhile, preheat oven to 375°F (190°C).

8. Bake rolls in preheated oven for 15 minutes. Brush again with some of the egg white mixture. Bake until golden brown and rolls sound hollow when tapped on the bottom, about 10 minutes. Transfer rolls to wire racks and let cool.

Variation

When I am pressed for time I use 1 lb (500 g) frozen bread dough. Thaw as directed and then divide dough into 10 portions, shape, let rise and bake as directed. However, bolillos are readily available at many local grocery stores in the bakery section.

Mexican Sweet Breads

Makes 12 buns	• Stand mixer with paddle attachment	
	• 2 baking sheets, lined with parchment paper	

Big sweet buns topped with sugary cinnamon are a treat found in most Mexican bakeries. Mexican sweet breads, or Conchas, which means "shells," are very easy to make but time-consuming. Be patient, then enjoy!

1	package (¼ oz/8 g) active dry yeast	1
½ cup	warm (100 to 110°F/38 to 43°C) water	125 mL
½ cup	warm evaporated milk (115 to 120°F/46 to 49°C)	125 mL
⅓ cup	granulated sugar	75 mL
⅓ cup	butter, melted, at room temperature	75 mL
2	large eggs	2
1 tsp	salt	5 mL
3 cups	all-purpose flour, divided	750 mL
1 tsp	ground cinnamon	5 mL
	Oil	

Topping

⅓ cup	butter, softened	75 mL
⅓ cup	granulated sugar	75 mL
1 tsp	vanilla extract	5 mL
⅓ cup	all-purpose flour (approx.)	75 mL
2 tsp	ground cinnamon	10 mL

1. In large mixer bowl, stir together yeast and warm water. Let stand until frothy, about 10 minutes.

2. In a smaller bowl, whisk together evaporated milk, sugar, melted butter, eggs and salt.

3. Attach bowl to mixer and fit with paddle attachment. On low speed, gradually beat milk mixture into yeast mixture. Mix in 2 cups (500 mL) of the flour. Beat in cinnamon, then gradually add enough of the remaining flour until dough just starts to pull away from the side of the bowl.

4. Place dough onto a lightly floured surface. Rub a small amount of oil on hands and knead dough until smooth and elastic, 3 to 5 minutes.

Tip

To make ahead, let cool completely and store in an airtight container and freeze for up to 3 months. Thaw at room temperature. Reheat in the microwave on Medium in 20 second intervals until warmed through.

5. Shape into a ball. Transfer dough to a large greased bowl and turn once to coat. Cover and let rise in a warm, draft-free place until doubled in size, 1 to $1\frac{1}{4}$ hours.

6. *Topping:* In a clean mixer bowl, using electric mixer on medium speed, beat butter, sugar and vanilla for 30 seconds. Gradually add flour and cinnamon and beat until smooth, about 4 minutes. Set aside.

7. Punch down dough. Divide dough into 12 equal portions and shape each portion into a smooth ball. Place balls 3 inches (7.5 cm) apart on prepared baking sheets. Flatten each ball to a round disk shape, about 2 inches (5 cm) thick and 3 inches (7.5 cm) in diameter.

8. Divide topping equally among 12 rolls, spreading across the top. Using a sharp paring knife, cut 3 or 4 grooves in topping to resemble the grooves on a scalloped sea shell. Cover rolls and let rise in a warm place until nearly doubled in size, about 45 minutes.

9. Meanwhile, preheat oven to 375°F (190°C).

10. Bake in preheated oven until golden brown and buns sound hollow when tapped on the bottom, 18 to 20 minutes. Transfer rolls to a wire rack and let cool slightly. Serve warm.

Variation

Delete cinnamon in the topping for a buttery variation.

Empanadas

|||||||||||||||||||||||||||||||||||||||||||||||||||||||||||||||||||||||||||||||||||||||||||||||

**Makes about
8 empanadas**

Empanadas are stuffed
Mexican turnovers
that can be filled with
sweet or savory fillings.
A simple fruit filling
makes a wonderful
dessert, yet a flavorful
meat filling can create
an appetizer everyone
will love.

Tips

Substitute solid vegetable
shortening for lard.

When I am pressed for
time, I use 15 oz (425 g)
store-bought pie pastry
dough. Continue with
Step 2.

To make ahead: Dough can
be refrigerated for up to
2 days. Follow Step 1 then
refrigerate for up to 2 days.
When ready to make, bring
dough to room temperature
and continue with Step 2.

Empanadas can be made
ahead. Let empanadas
cool completely and store
in an airtight container and
freeze for up to 3 months.
Thaw at room temperature.
Wrap in foil and reheat in
a preheated 200°F (100°C)
oven until heated through,
12 to 15 minutes.

- Preheat oven to 375°F (190°C)
- 6-inch (15 cm) round cookie cutter
- Baking sheet, greased

2 cups	all-purpose flour	500 mL
2 tsp	baking powder	10 mL
¼ tsp	salt	1 mL
⅓ cup	lard (see Tips, left)	75 mL
¼ cup	milk	60 mL
1¼ cups	Savory or Sweet Filling (see Variations, below)	300 mL
1	egg, beaten	1

1. In a large bowl, combine flour, baking powder and salt. Using a pastry blender or two knives, cut in lard until well blended and dough is crumbly. Add milk, 1 tbsp (15 mL) at a time, and knead to form dough into a ball. Place dough in a resealable plastic bag.

2. Place ⅓ of the dough onto a lightly floured surface. Roll out to ⅛-inch (3 mm) thickness. Cut circles with cookie cutter, re-rolling scraps.

3. Place 2½ tbsp (37 mL) filling in the center of each circle. Dampen edges of the pastry with water and fold over to make a half-moon shape. Pinch the edges to seal. Brush tops with egg. Repeat with remaining dough and filling.

4. Bake in preheated oven until golden brown and filling is hot, 14 to 16 minutes. Let cool slightly and serve warm.

Variations

Savory Filling: In a bowl, combine 2 tbsp (30 mL) Salsa Verde (page 58) and 1¼ cups (300 mL) cooked ground beef seasoned with salt and pepper, drained.

Sweet Filling: Add 1 tbsp (15 mL) granulated sugar in Step 1 for the empanada dough. Continue with Steps 1 and 2. Strain most of the liquid from 1½ cups (375 mL) canned apple or peach pie filling, reserving liquid in a bowl. Chop fruit pieces finely, then stir back into liquid in bowl.

Sopapillas

|||||||||||||||||||||||||||||||||||||||||||||||||||||||||||||||||||||||||||||||||||||||||||||

**Makes about
16 sopapillas**

These fresh, crispy
pastry puffs are so
delicious and versatile.
I like to tear a corner
off of this little quick
bread and drizzle honey
in the center or dust
with sugar. They are
also delicious stuffed
with savory fillings for
a delicious entrée.

Tips

If dough seems crumbly,
after the ¼ cup (60 mL) milk
is added, add 1 tbsp (15 mL)
more milk to make a smooth
dough.

Sopapillas are best when
eaten immediately when
they are fresh and warm.

For the best results in frying
up the sopapillas, use a
large long-handled spoon,
splash oil over the top of
each sopapilla once you
have turned them. This will
make them puff up and be
hollow in the middle.

- Stand mixer with paddle attachment
- Candy/deep-fry thermometer

3 cups	all-purpose flour	750 mL
2 tsp	baking powder	10 mL
1 tsp	salt	5 mL
½ cup	warm water	125 mL
½ cup	shortening	125 mL
¼ cup	milk (see Tips, left)	60 mL
	Oil	
	Honey	
	Confectioner's (icing) sugar	

1. In a large mixer bowl, combine flour, baking powder and salt. Attach bowl to stand mixer and fit with paddle attachment. On low speed, gradually beat in warm water and shortening. Mix for 2 minutes. Continue to mix and gradually add milk until dough is well blended, stiff and not sticky to the touch. Transfer to a resealable plastic bag and let stand for 30 minutes.

2. Place half of the dough onto a lightly floured surface. Roll out to ⅛-inch (3 mm) thickness. With a knife, cut into 5-inch (12.5 cm) squares. Repeat with remaining dough.

3. Fill a deep fryer, deep heavy pot or large deep skillet with 3 inches (7.5 cm) of oil and heat to 350°F (180°C). Using tongs, fry 2 squares at a time, turning once, until they create air pockets and are golden brown, about 2 minutes. Drain on paper towels. Serve with honey or dust with confectioner's sugar. Serve warm.

Variation

For a sweeter flavor, add 1 tbsp (15 mL) granulated sugar in Step 1.

Fry Bread

Makes 8 fry breads

This flat, leavened dough is deep-fried. The soft-crust bread is typically piled high with pinto beans and fresh produce, creating an open-faced taco delight. It is also delicious brushed with butter and dusted with confectioner's sugar.

Tip

Fry bread is best when eaten immediately when it is fresh and warm.

● Candy/deep-fry thermometer

3 cups	all-purpose flour	750 mL
2 tsp	baking soda	10 mL
1 tsp	salt	5 mL
¾ cup	water	175 mL
½ cup	butter, melted	125 mL
	Oil	

1. In a large bowl, combine flour, baking soda and salt. Gradually add water and butter, stirring, until dough comes together. In the bowl, knead with your hands just until dough is smooth.

2. Place dough onto a floured surface and divide dough into 8 equal portions. Rub a small amount of oil onto hands and shape each portion of dough into a 6-inch (15 cm) flat round. Cover rounds with a clean towel and set aside.

3. Fill a deep fryer, deep heavy pot or large deep skillet with 3 inches (7.5 cm) of oil and heat to 350°F (180°C). Using tongs, fry one dough round at a time, turning once, until golden brown, about 2 minutes. Drain on paper towels. Let cool slightly.

Variation

For a sweet bread, dust each round with confectioner's (icing) sugar. For a savory taco, top each fry bread with ¼ cup (60 mL) Basic Pinto Beans (page 99) and garnish with equal amounts of shredded lettuce, diced tomato and shredded cheeses.

Soups and Stews

Chicken Tortilla Soup

	Makes 4 to	
	6 servings	

This soup is all about layering flavor upon flavor. This family favorite starts with a basic chicken soup that is then accented with tortilla chips, creamy cheese, a little chile pepper, onions and tomatoes. Everyone can garnish the way they would like and enjoy.

2 tbsp	butter	30 mL
1	medium onion, chopped	1
2	cloves garlic, minced	2
¾ cup	chopped roasted green chile peppers (see page 98)	175 mL
6 cups	chicken broth	1.5 L
⅓ cup	tomato juice	75 mL
2 cups	shredded cooked chicken breasts (page 153)	500 mL
2 cups	broken corn tortilla chips	500 mL
2 cups	shredded Monterey Jack cheese	500 mL
1 tbsp	hot pepper flakes or to taste	15 mL
4	green onions, green parts only, minced	4
2	tomatoes, seeded and diced	2
2 tbsp	minced cilantro	30 mL
¾ cup	sour cream	175 mL

1. In a large pot, melt butter over medium heat. Add onion, garlic and chiles. Cover and cook, stirring occasionally, until onion is transparent, 8 to 10 minutes.

2. Add broth, tomato juice and chicken. Reduce heat to low. Cover and simmer for 15 minutes.

3. To serve, divide chips equally among serving bowls and ladle soup over chips. Top with cheese. Garnish each bowl with a pinch of hot pepper flakes, green onions, tomatoes and cilantro. Top each bowl with a dollop of sour cream.

Variations

Spicy Chicken: For a spicy chicken tortilla soup, omit green chiles, tomato juice and shredded chicken and use Spicy Chicken instead. In a small bowl, combine ½ tsp (2 mL) ground cumin, ½ tsp (2 mL) chili powder, ½ tsp (2 mL) garlic powder and pinch of salt. Cut 2 boneless skinless chicken breasts horizontally into 2 thin slices. Rub chicken pieces with 2 tbsp (30 mL) olive oil. Season each breast with cumin mixture. Pan fry over medium-high heat, turning once, until chicken is no longer pink inside and golden brown, 8 to 10 minutes. Dice chicken and add to broth.

Chicken and Lime Soup

**Makes 4 to
6 servings**

There is a light citrusy flavor that you will love in this hearty chicken soup. Layers of garlic and lime embrace the fresh avocado garnish. I serve this during the warm summer months.

Tip

You can use the recipe for Poached Chicken (page 153) here instead of the boneless skinless chicken breast. Skip Step 1 and continue with Step 2.

2 tbsp	olive oil, divided	30 mL
4	boneless skinless chicken breasts (see Tip, left)	4
1 cup	chopped onion	250 mL
2	cloves garlic, minced	2
2	tomatoes, seeded and chopped	2
6 cups	chicken broth	1.5 L
½ cup	freshly squeezed lime juice (4 to 5 limes)	125 mL
2 cups	broken corn tortilla chips	500 mL
2	avocados, diced	2
4	green onions, green parts only, minced	4

1. In a large skillet, heat 1 tbsp (15 mL) of the oil over medium-high heat. Add chicken and cook, turning once, until no longer pink inside, 6 to 8 minutes per side. Transfer chicken to a cutting board and let cool.

2. In a large pot, heat remaining oil over medium heat. Add onion, garlic and tomatoes. Cover and cook until onion is softened, 4 to 6 minutes. Add chicken broth and lime juice.

3. Dice chicken and add to pot. Cover and bring to a boil over medium heat. Reduce heat to low and simmer for 10 minutes. Ladle into individual bowls and garnish with equal amounts of tortilla chips, avocado and green onion.

Mexican Meatball Soup

Makes 6 to 8 servings		

Sopa de Albondigas is the Mexican version of comfort food. Tender little meatballs (*albondigas* means "meatball" in Spanish) linger in a flavorful broth, satisfying the hungriest appetites.

Meatballs

1 lb	ground beef, preferably sirloin	500 g
2 tbsp	long-grain white rice	30 mL
1	large egg	1
¼ cup	fresh oregano leaves, minced	60 mL
1 tsp	salt	5 mL
1 tsp	freshly ground black pepper	5 mL
1 tsp	olive oil	5 mL
1 cup	diced onion	250 mL
4	cloves garlic, minced	4
8 cups	beef broth (see Tip, right)	2 L
2 tbsp	tomato paste	30 mL
1	carrot, peeled and sliced	1
2 tbsp	minced cilantro	30 mL

1. *Meatballs:* In a large bowl, combine meat, rice and egg. Mix in oregano, salt and pepper. Roll into 1-inch (2.5 cm) balls.

2. In a large pot, heat oil over medium-low heat Add onion and cook, stirring, until softened, 3 to 5 minutes. Add garlic and cook, stirring, for 2 minutes. Add broth and tomato paste. Increase heat to medium-high. Bring to a boil. Add carrot and cook until carrots are soft, 20 to 30 minutes. Reduce heat to a simmer.

Tip

Beef broth can be high in sodium. Use reduced-sodium broth instead.

3. Gently add meatballs to simmering broth. Cover and simmer until meatballs are no longer pink inside and rice is tender, about 30 minutes. Ladle into individual bowls. Garnish with cilantro.

Variations

Many Mexican cooks use mint in the meatballs. You can omit the oregano and add $1/4$ cup (60 mL) mint, minced, $1/4$ cup (60 mL) cilantro, minced; or for less flavor but good color, $1/4$ cup (60 mL) Italian flat-leaf parsley, minced.

Follow Step 2 and add 1 potato, diced into bite-size pieces, with the carrots.

Menudo

||||||||||||||||||||||||||||||||||||||||||||||||||||||||||||||||||||||||||||||||||||||||||||||||

Makes 4 to 6 servings

Menudo is a traditional Mexican soup that is said to be a cure for hangovers. This slow cooked beef stomach in a clear broth is tasty and aromatic.

||||||||||||||||||||||||||||||||||||||||||

Tip

Mexican oregano has a bit of a citrusy flavor. It is coarse and flaky in texture. Substitute 1 tsp (5 mL) traditional oregano for 2 tsp (10 mL) Mexican oregano.

2 lbs	beef tripe, uncut	1 kg
2	onions, chopped, divided	2
3	cloves garlic, minced	3
2 tsp	whole Mexican oregano (see Tip, left)	10 mL
1 tbsp	salt	15 mL
1	can (28 oz/796 mL) white hominy, drained	1
½ cup	chopped cilantro	125 mL
1 tbsp	hot pepper flakes	15 mL
2	limes, each cut into 4 wedges	2

1. Rinse tripe well under cold running water and pat dry.

2. In a large pot over medium heat, combine tripe, half of the onions, garlic, oregano and salt. Add enough water to cover. Bring to a boil. Boil for 20 minutes.

3. Reduce heat and simmer until tripe is tender, about 1½ hours.

4. Using tongs, carefully remove tripe and transfer to a cutting board. Cut into bite-size pieces. Return to pot and add hominy. Simmer for 1 hour.

5. Serve in individual bowls. Garnish with remaining onion and cilantro. Sprinkle with hot pepper flakes and serve with lime wedges.

Variations

For a slightly different taste and texture, substitute 2 lbs (1 kg) boneless beef sirloin, trimmed and cut into ½-inch (1 cm) pieces, for the tripe.

Menudo Colorado: For a rich chile flavor, add 1 cup (250 mL) Red Enchilada Sauce (page 63) to the hominy and meat mixture.

Crème Chile and Corn Chowder

Makes 6 to 8 servings

I created this creamy chowder to reflect the flavors of *calabacitas*, a traditional Mexican side dish full of zucchini and squash.

3 tbsp	butter	45 mL
3	cloves garlic, minced	3
2	cans (each 14 to 15 oz/398 to 425 mL) corn kernels, drained	2
2	large zucchini, chopped into 1/4-inch (0.5 cm) pieces	2
1 cup	chopped roasted green chile peppers (see page 98)	250 mL
2	cans (each 15 oz/425 mL or three, each 10 oz/284 mL) condensed cheese soup	2
2 1/2 cups	half-and-half (10%) cream	625 mL
1 cup	shredded Cheddar cheese	250 mL

1. In a large skillet, melt butter over medium heat. Add garlic, corn, zucchini and chiles and cook, stirring often, until zucchini starts to soften, 10 to 12 minutes. Set aside.

2. In a large pot, combine condensed soup and cream. Reduce heat and simmer, stirring occasionally, for 12 to 14 minutes.

3. Add corn mixture to chowder. Simmer, stirring, until heated through, 10 to 12 minutes. Serve in individual bowls and garnish with cheese.

Variation

Substitute 8 oz (250 g) processed cheese spread, such as Velveeta, cubed, and an additional 1 cup (250 mL) half-and-half (10%) cream for the condensed cheese soup.

Red Chile Pork Posole

Makes 6 to 8 servings

Posole is a regional favorite. Historically it is a ceremonial dish that celebrates life's blessings. It is a combination of hearty pork, hominy and spicy red chile. Garnish with fresh lime, radishes and green onion.

Tips

I like using canned hominy due to the texture.

You can buy dried Mexican oregano in the international food section of your grocery store, but if it's not available substitute 1½ tsp (7 mL) regular dried oregano.

2 lbs	boneless pork shoulder blade (butt) roast, cubed	1 kg
3 cups	white hominy, canned, drained and rinsed (see Tips, left)	750 mL
2 tbsp	salt	30 mL
4	cloves garlic, minced	4
1 tbsp	dried Mexican oregano (see Tips, left)	15 mL
1½ tsp	ground cumin	7 mL
1½ cups	Red Enchilada Sauce (page 63) or store-bought	375 mL
2½ cups	water	625 mL
5	green onions, green parts only, chopped	5
5 to 7	radishes, sliced	5 to 7
½ cup	minced cilantro	125 mL
2	lemons, quartered	2

1. Place pork in a large pot. Add just enough water to cover. Bring to a boil over medium-high heat. Reduce heat and boil gently, stirring occasionally, until pork is tender and water and juices have evaporated, 2 to 3 hours. Reduce heat to low.

2. Stir in hominy, salt, garlic, oregano, cumin and sauce, mixing well. Slowly stir in water. Simmer, stirring occasionally, until completely heated through, 10 to 12 minutes.

3. Ladle into individual bowls and garnish with green onions, radishes to taste, cilantro and a wedge of lemon.

Green Chile Shrimp Posole

**Makes 6 to
8 servings**

This is my version of a
wonderful posole my
friend Louis serves up
every holiday season.
However, it is light and
delicious and can be
served year round. The
shrimp and hominy is a
delicious combination
of flavor.

Tip

Hominy can be found in the
Mexican food section of
your grocery store or online.

6 cups	water	1.5 L
1 lb	medium shrimp, in the shell	500 g
1 tbsp	olive oil	15 mL
3	cloves garlic, minced	3
1	onion, chopped	1
1 cup	chopped roasted green chile peppers (see page 98)	250 mL
2 cups	chicken broth	500 mL
1	can (36.5 oz/1 kg) hominy, drained (see Tip, left)	1
2	sprigs fresh oregano	2
2 tbsp	minced cilantro	30 mL
1	onion, chopped	1
7 to 10	radishes	7 to 10
3	limes, cut in wedges	3

1. In a large pot of boiling water, boil shrimp until shrimp turn opaque and pink, 10 to 12 minutes. Drain, shrimp, reserving liquid. Set aside.

2. In another large pot, heat oil over medium heat. Add garlic and cook, stirring, until tender, about 1 minute. Add onion and chiles and cook, stirring, until onion is translucent, 4 to 6 minutes. Increase heat to medium-high. Add reserved shrimp liquid and chicken broth and bring to a boil.

3. Peel shrimp and add to soup with hominy. Reduce heat and simmer just until heated through, about 20 minutes. Ladle into bowls and garnish with cilantro, onion, radishes and/or limes.

Green Chile Stew

Makes 6 to 8 servings

This hearty stew is a Mexican favorite. Serve it up in bowls with tortillas on the side or wrap it in a fresh flour tortilla for a saucy burrito.

Tip

The lard gives this taco an authentic Mexican flavor. Substitute solid vegetable shortening for the lard, if you prefer, but the taste will be different.

3 lb	boneless beef top sirloin roast, cut into 1-inch (2.5 cm) cubes	1.5 kg
¼ cup	lard (see Tip, left)	60 mL
1	onion, chopped	1
3 cups	chopped roasted green chile peppers (see page 98)	750 mL
1	can (28 oz (796 mL) diced tomatoes with juice	1
4	cloves garlic, minced	4
	Kosher salt	
1 tbsp	coarsely ground black pepper	15 mL

1. Place beef in a large pot. Add just enough water to cover. Bring to a boil over medium-high heat. Cook, stirring, until browned and juices have evaporated, 1 to 2 hours.

2. In a large saucepan, melt lard over medium heat. Add onion and cook, stirring, until soft, 8 to 10 minutes. Add chiles and tomatoes with juice and boil gently, stirring occasionally.

3. Add tomato mixture to meat. Stir in garlic, salt to taste and pepper. Reduce heat and simmer, stirring occasionally and adjusting heat as necessary, until thickened, 1 to 2 hours.

Beefy Mexican Vegetable Stew

Makes 6 servings

Caldillo is a Mexican version of beef stew. It has a thick flavorful broth and is filled with good hearty vegetables.

2 lb	boneless beef top sirloin or round, cut into bite-size cubes	1 kg
1 tbsp	garlic powder	15 mL
1 tbsp	onion powder	15 mL
1 tsp	ground cumin	5 mL
1	can (14 to 15 oz/398 to 425 mL) diced tomatoes with juice	1
4 cups	beef broth	1 L
2 cups	chicken broth	500 mL
¾ cup	chopped roasted green chile peppers (see page 98)	175 mL
2	potatoes, cut into bite-size pieces	2
	Salt and freshly ground black pepper	
2	cobs corn, each cut crosswise into 4 pieces	2

1. Place beef in a large pot. Add just enough water to cover. Bring to a boil over medium-high heat. Cook, stirring, until all water and juices have evaporated and beef is tender, 1 to 2 hours.

2. Add garlic powder, onion powder and cumin to the meat and stir until meat is well coated.

3. Add tomatoes with juice and beef and chicken broths. Bring to a boil over medium heat. Stir in chiles and potatoes. Season with salt and pepper to taste. Boil until potatoes are soft, about 15 minutes. Add corn and cook for 15 minutes more.

Fresh Green Chile and Pinto Beans

Makes 6 to 8 servings

This is my favorite quick pot of beans. They are so comforting on a cold day. The perfect combination of pintos and green chile accented with ham.

Tips

Substitute vegetable or canola oil for lard. The lard gives this pot of beans an authentic Mexican flavor. Substitute solid vegetable shortening for the lard, if you prefer, but the taste will be different.

When I am pressed for time, I substitute 3 cans (each 14 to 19 oz/398 to 540 mL) pinto beans with liquid for the 6 cups (1.5 L) cooked pinto beans.

2 tbsp	lard	30 mL
2	cloves garlic, minced	2
1	onion, sliced into rings	1
¾ cup	chopped roasted green chile peppers (see page 98)	175 mL
6 cups	cooked Basic Pinto Beans with liquid (see page 99 and Tips, left)	1.5 L
1½ cups	diced lean cooked ham	375 mL
	Salt	

1. In a large pot, melt lard over medium-high heat. Sauté garlic, onion and chiles until onion is softened, 4 to 6 minutes.

2. Add beans with liquid and ham and bring to a boil. Boil, until ham is heated through, 6 to 8 minutes. Reduce heat, cover and simmer, stirring occasionally, for at least 30 minutes and up to 4 hours. If beans get too dry, add more liquid. Serve in individual bowls.

Vegetables, Beans and Salads

Creamy Corn, Chile and Squash

Makes 4 to 6 servings

Calabacitas is a traditional Mexican corn and squash dish full of texture. It is a mellow combination of corn, chile and squash blended together with creamy goodness.

Tips

Increase zucchini to 2 cups (500 mL) if summer squash is out of season or hard.

Drained canned or thawed frozen corn kernels work in this recipe. Grilled or fire-roasted corn will add additional flavor.

The salt in the broth and cheese will add flavor. However, salt to taste if more is needed.

1 tbsp	olive oil	15 mL
½ cup	chopped onion	125 mL
2	cloves garlic, minced	2
1 cup	chopped summer squash (see Tips, left)	250 mL
2 cups	chopped zucchini	500 mL
1 tbsp	minced flat-leaf parsley	15 mL
2 cups	cooked corn kernels (see Tips, left)	500 mL
1 cup	shredded Monterey Jack cheese	250 mL
2 tbsp	chicken broth	30 mL
	Freshly ground black pepper to taste	

1. In a large skillet, heat oil over medium-high heat. Sauté onion, garlic, summer squash, zucchini and parsley until vegetables are tender-crisp, 10 to 12 minutes.

2. Reduce heat to low and stir in corn, cheese and broth until cheese is melted and mixture is heated through, 6 to 8 minutes. Pour into a serving dish.

Variations

For a spicy flavor, add ½ cup (125 mL) roasted Anaheim or New Mexico green chile (see page 98) in Step 1. Continue with Step 2.

For a casserole style–dish, preheat oven to 350°F (180°C). Follow Step 1 and pour into a greased 8-inch (20 cm) square glass baking dish. Top with ½ cup (125 mL) grated Cheddar cheese, then lightly sprinkle with ½ cup (125 mL) bread crumbs. Bake for 20 minutes until cheese is melted and bubbly.

Spanish Rice

Makes 4 to
6 servings

Spanish rice is a traditional side dish that is loaded with flavor. Garlic, onion and tomato accent the rice and create a light, easy side.

Tips

If rice does not have a soft texture, reduce heat and cook, covered, for another 5 to 10 minutes, being careful not to burn the rice on the bottom of pan.

If rice does have a soft texture but liquid remains in pan, continue cooking rice, uncovered, until liquid has evaporated.

2 tbsp	light olive oil	30 mL
½ cup	chopped onion	125 mL
3	cloves garlic, minced	3
1¼ cups	long-grain white rice	300 mL
3 cups	water	750 mL
1 cup	tomato sauce	250 mL
	Salt	

1. In a large skillet, heat oil over medium heat. Sauté onion and garlic until onion is transparent, 4 to 6 minutes. Add rice and sauté until rice starts to brown lightly, 4 to 6 minutes.

2. Add water and tomato sauce and blend well. Bring to a boil. Reduce heat to medium-low. Cover and simmer until rice is tender and liquid has evaporated, 15 to 20 minutes. Fluff rice with a fork. Season with salt to taste.

Green Chile and Herb Rice

Makes 4 to 6 servings

Flavors of fresh green chile and cilantro team up for a rice dish that is unforgettable.

● Food processor

½ cup	chopped roasted green chile peppers (see below)	125 mL
½ cup	minced fresh cilantro	125 mL
2	cloves garlic, minced	2
3 tbsp	olive oil	45 mL
2 cups	cooked white or brown rice	500 mL

1. In a food processor, combine chiles, cilantro, garlic and oil and process until smooth with a little texture, 1 to 2 minutes.

2. In a large microwave-safe bowl, combine rice and chile mixture. Mix well. Cover with plastic wrap and microwave on High for 1 minute. Remove and stir. Repeat until rice is heated through, 3 to 4 minutes.

Roasting Chiles

To roast chiles, such as New Mexico, Anaheim, poblano, jalapeño and habanero: Preheat greased outdoor grill to medium or preheat an oven broiler. Place fresh chiles on outdoor grill or gas stove top over medium heat or arrange on a baking sheet and place 2 to 3 inches (5 to 7.5 cm) away from heat under broiler. Grill or broil, turning often with tongs, until surfaces of skin are lightly charred and blistered. Immediately place peppers in a paper bag, or an airtight container and close tightly. Let peppers cool for 12 to 15 minutes. Peel off charred skin and remove stems and seeds. Tear into strips or chop as needed according to the recipe. Wash your hands thoroughly after handling chiles. Refrigerate peppers for up to 3 days or freeze in airtight container for up to 6 months.

Basic Pinto Beans

Makes 6 cups (1.5 L)		

3 cups	dried pinto beans	750 mL
1 tbsp	garlic powder	15 mL
1 tbsp	onion powder	15 mL

Beans are one of the most important elements of the Mexican cuisine. Dried beans have always been a staple of the Mexican diet. Pinto, black and kidney beans are all favorites. This simple recipe of basic pinto beans can be used in salads, soups and refried bean dishes.

Tips

Test beans by smashing one bean between thumb and index finger.

Store beans in an airtight container and refrigerate for up to 2 days or freeze for up to 4 months.

1. Place beans, garlic powder and onion powder in a large pot. Add enough water to cover by 4 inches (10 cm) and bring to a boil over medium-high heat. Reduce heat and boil gently until soft (see Tips, left), $2\frac{1}{2}$ to 3 hours. Let cool completely to room temperature, about 2 to 3 hours.

Variation

Substitute black beans or kidney beans for the pinto beans. Follow Step 1.

Stove Top Refried Beans

Makes 2 cups (500 mL)		

Refried beans can be done quickly. A true authentic Mexican flavor is best achieved by refrying these beans in lard. They are delicious.

2 cups	cooked pinto beans, drained reserving liquid (page 99)	500 mL
2 tbsp	lard	30 mL
	Salt	

1. In a large skillet, heat beans and ¼ cup (60 mL) reserved liquid over medium-high heat. Bring to a boil and boil for 2 minutes. Reduce heat to medium-low. Using a potato masher, gently mash beans. Beans should be like a thick paste, not runny. If too thick, add more reserved liquid, 1 tsp (5 mL) at a time, until bean mixture is thick, but not stiff. Repeat until all beans are mashed.

2. In another large skillet, melt lard over medium-high heat. Add mashed beans and stir until well blended and bubbly, 4 to 6 minutes. Season with salt to taste.

> ## Variations
> Substitute 2 tbsp (30 mL) vegetable or canola oil for lard.
>
> *Quick Refried Beans:* Substitute 2 cans (each 14 to 19 oz/398 to 540 mL) pinto beans. Follow Steps 1 and 2.

Baked Chile Rellenos

Makes 4 to 6 servings

This is a casserole-style dish that highlights the combination of green chiles and melted cheese. It is a simple way to get the flavor of traditional rellenos (rey~e~nos) without individually frying each one.

Tip

If you cannot find fresh chiles, substitute 2 cans (each 27 oz/765 mL) whole roasted green chiles, depending on how many chiles they contain.

- Preheat oven 350°F (180°C)
- 13- by 9-inch (33 by 23 cm) glass baking dish, greased

24	whole New Mexico or Anaheim green chiles, roasted and peeled (see Tips, left, and page 98)	24
1 lb	Cheddar cheese, shredded	500 g
1 lb	Monterey Jack cheese, shredded	500 g
½ cup	all-purpose flour	125 mL
½ tsp	baking powder	2 mL
8	large eggs	8
1 cup	whole milk	250 mL
1 tsp	salt	5 mL

1. In a medium bowl, combine Cheddar and Monterey Jack cheeses, mixing well. On a cutting board, carefully slice each chile, making a slit down one side lengthwise and remove seeds and stem. Place 1 to 2 tbsp (15 to 30 mL) cheese mixture in each chile. Place stuffed chiles on the bottom of prepared baking dish.

2. In another medium bowl, combine flour and baking powder. In a separate medium bowl, whisk eggs until lemony in color. Add milk and blend well.

3. Slowly add egg mixture and salt to dry ingredients. Using an electric mixer, beat until light and fluffy, 2 to 3 minutes. Pour equally over chiles.

4. Bake in preheated oven until center is firm and edges are slightly browned, 35 to 45 minutes. Let stand for 5 minutes before serving.

Traditional Chile Rellenos

Makes 8 servings		

Lightly breaded chiles stuffed with creamy cheese are sure to please. This Mexican favorite takes time but is worth the effort. They can be served as a side dish or as the main entrée.

Tip

Rellenos can be made ahead and frozen in a resealable plastic freezer bag for up to 3 months. Thaw at room temperature and reheat at 200°F (100°C).

● Candy/deep-fry thermometer

8	whole Anahiem or New Mexico green chiles, roasted and peeled (see page 98)	8
4 oz	Cheddar cheese, cut into 8 slices	125 g
4 oz	Monterey Jack cheese, cut into 8 slices	125 g
1¾ cups	all-purpose flour, divided	425 mL
3	large eggs, beaten	3
¼ cup	water	60 mL
1 tsp	baking powder	5 mL
	Oil	

1. On a cutting board, carefully slice each chile lengthwise near the stem, leaving seeds and stem. Gently stuff each chile with 1 slice of each cheese. Spread 1 cup (250 mL) of the flour on a plate. Roll stuffed chile in flour and set aside.

2. In a medium bowl, whisk together eggs and water. Slowly mix in remaining ¾ cup (175 mL) flour and baking powder. Using an electric mixer, beat until smooth, about 4 minutes.

3. In a deep pot or Dutch oven, heat oil over medium-high heat until temperature reaches 375°F (190°C). Using tongs, dip each chile in batter, letting excess drip off, and gently place in oil, 2 or 3 at a time. Fry, turning once, until golden brown, 3 to 4 minutes per side. Drain on paper towels. Serve warm.

> ## Variation
>
> Serve smothered with Green Enchilada Sauce (page 64), Red Enchilada Sauce (page 63) or Sonoran Enchilada Sauce (page 65).

Spicy Squash and Zucchini Bake

**Makes 4 to
6 servings**

Fresh vegetables and
a hint of chile pepper
from your favorite
salsa make a delicious
combination. This
casserole-style side dish
can be prepared quickly
and with ease.

Tip

If you are pressed for
time, substitute prepared
tomato-based salsa.

- Preheat oven 375°F (190°C)
- 13- by 9-inch (33 by 23 cm) greased glass baking dish

2 lbs	yellow squash, washed and cut into ½-inch (1 cm) slices	1 kg
2 lbs	zucchini, washed and cut into ½-inch (1 cm) slices	1 kg
1½ cups	Tomato Table Salsa (page 57)	375 mL
1½ cups	shredded Monterey Jack cheese	375 mL
2 tbsp	butter, melted	30 mL
½ cup	dried bread crumbs	125 mL

1. Arrange squash and zucchini in baking dish. Spoon salsa equally over top of vegetables. Top with cheese.

2. In a small bowl, combine melted butter and bread crumbs. Sprinkle equally over cheese. Cover with foil.

3. Bake in preheated oven until vegetables are soft and cheese is melted and bubbly, about 20 minutes. Remove foil and bake until golden brown, 8 to 10 minutes more. Serve with a slotted spoon in the event that moisture has collected along the bottom of the pan.

Variation
Add fresh herbs such as ¼ cup (60 mL) cilantro for additional flavor in Step 1. Then continue with Step 2.

Spicy Fresh Greens

**Makes 4 to
6 servings**

This easy salad pairs
well with enchiladas,
tacos and burritos.
Zesty spices, color and
citrus flavor satisfy the
senses.

Tip

My family loves the Lemon
Vinaigrette so I often double
the recipe.

6 cups	mixed greens	1.5 L
1½ cups	hearts of palm, drained and sliced	375 mL
1	medium red onion, sliced into rings	1
1	red bell pepper, seeded and cored, sliced into strips	1

Lemon Vinaigrette

⅓ cup	olive oil	75 mL
¼ cup	freshly squeezed lemon juice	60 mL
1 tsp	dried dillweed	5 mL
1 tsp	hot pepper flakes	5 mL
1	clove garlic, minced	1

1. In a large bowl, gently toss together mixed greens, hearts of palm, red onion and bell pepper. Refrigerate for 30 minutes or for up to 4 hours.

2. *Lemon Vinaigrette:* In a small glass bowl, whisk together olive oil, lemon juice, dill, hot pepper flakes and garlic. Whisk until well blended. Toss vinaigrette with chilled greens and serve.

Red Chile Potatoes

**Makes 4 to
6 servings**

This hearty dish is
so versatile. It can be
served for breakfast,
lunch or dinner. The
red chile complements
the potatoes with a
little kick.

Tip

If you are pressed for time
you can skip Step 1. Follow
Step 2. Cook, stirring
occasionally, until golden
brown and crispy, 18 to
20 minutes.

- Preheat oven to 375°F (190°C)
- Ovenproof serving platter or baking dish

4	medium baking potatoes (unpeeled), cut into 1-inch (2.5 cm)	4
2 tbsp	vegetable oil	30 mL
1 tsp	seasoned salt	5 mL
1½ cups	Red Enchilada Sauce, warmed (page 63) or store-bought	375 mL
1 cup	shredded Cheddar cheese	250 mL

1. Fill a large pot half full of water and bring to a boil over medium-high heat. Carefully and gently add potato cubes and boil until tender but firm, 14 to 16 minutes. Drain thoroughly.

2. In a skillet, heat oil over medium-high heat. Add potatoes and season with salt. Cook, stirring occasionally, until golden brown and crispy, 8 to 10 minutes.

3. Place potatoes on ovenproof serving platter. Top equally with enchilada sauce and cheese. Bake in preheated oven until potatoes are heated through and cheese is melted, 20 to 25 minutes.

Variation

To add more flavor, follow Steps 1 and 2. Place potatoes on ovenproof serving platter. Top with 4 oz (125 g) sausage or ground beef, cooked and crumbled. Continue with Step 3.

Green Chile Mashed Potatoes

Makes 4 servings

Creamy mashed potatoes and green chiles come together to create a new flavorful side dish. I like to serve these with my Spicy Steak Tampico (page 165) for a Mexican twist on a traditional dinner.

4	medium baking potatoes, peeled and cut into 1-inch (2.5 cm) cubes	4
¼ cup	butter, divided	60 mL
½ cup	milk, warmed	125 mL
3	cloves garlic, minced	3
¾ cup	chopped roasted green chile peppers (page 98)	175 mL
	Kosher salt	

1. Fill a large pot half full of water and bring to a boil over medium-high heat. Carefully and gently add potato cubes and boil until tender, 16 to 18 minutes. Drain thoroughly. Let cool slightly.

2. Mash potatoes with 3 tbsp (45 mL) of the butter and milk until smooth.

3. In a skillet over medium heat, melt remaining 1 tbsp (15 mL) butter. Add garlic and chiles and cook until garlic is soft, 4 to 6 minutes. Fold garlic chile mixture into potatoes until well blended. Season to taste with salt.

Variation

You can leave the skin on the potatoes. Just use two sharp knives to dice potatoes a bit smaller before mashing them.

Festive Mexican Slaw

Makes 4 to
6 servings

A simple coleslaw marinated with tangy vinegar is perfect for any Mexican meal. I serve this as a side dish or as garnish for tacos, tortas or enchiladas.

Tip

For a different flavor, substitute olive oil for the canola oil.

½ cup	canola oil	125 mL
⅓ cup	white vinegar	75 mL
½ tsp	salt	2 mL
3 cups	finely shredded green cabbage	750 mL
2 cups	finely shredded red cabbage	500 mL
⅓ cup	diced red bell pepper	75 mL
	Cracked black peppercorns	

1. In a large bowl, whisk together oil, vinegar and salt until well blended. Add green and red cabbage and bell pepper and toss until well coated. Season with pepper to taste. Transfer to an airtight container and refrigerate, stirring occasionally, for up to 1 hour before serving. Coleslaw will keep, covered and refrigerated, for up to 2 days.

Variations

For a simpler version, omit red cabbage and red bell pepper and use 5 cups (1.25 L) green cabbage instead.

For additional flavor, add juice of 1 lime.

Chopped Mexican Salad

Makes 4 to 6 servings

Fresh goodness and color are at the heart of this fresh chopped salad. A citrus marinade refreshes these chopped veggies. This is a wonderful vegetarian meal but can be topped with chicken or steak as well.

Tips

Instead of canned corn, you can use 1½ cups (375 mL) thawed frozen corn kernels or cooked fresh corn in this recipe. Grilled or fire-roasted corn will add additional flavor.

Cotija is a crumbly, sharp Mexican cheese. You could substitute feta or goat cheese.

Dressing is best served at room temperature.

Dressing

½ cup	freshly squeezed lime juice	125 mL
⅓ cup	olive oil	75 mL
1 tbsp	minced cilantro	15 mL
1 tsp	hot pepper flakes	5 mL
2	cloves garlic, minced	2
2 tbsp	liquid honey	30 mL
6 cups	chopped romaine lettuce	1.5 L
1	can (14 to 19 oz/398 to 540 mL) black or pinto beans, rinsed and drained	1
1 cup	chopped peeled jicama	250 mL
1	can (14 to 15 oz/398 to 425 mL) corn kernels, drained (see Tips, left)	1
1	yellow or red bell pepper, seeded, cored and diced	1
2	ripe avocados, peeled and diced	2
½ cup	crumbled Cotija cheese (see Tips, left)	125 mL

1. *Dressing:* In a small bowl, whisk together lime juice, olive oil, cilantro, hot pepper flakes, garlic and honey.

2. Spread lettuce evenly across a large serving platter. Arrange beans, jicama, corn, bell pepper and avocado side by side on top of lettuce. Garnish with cheese. Cover and refrigerate until chilled, for at least 1 hour before serving.

3. Drizzle with dressing before serving.

Variation

Mexican Chopped Chicken Salad: To grill chicken: Preheat greased barbecue grill to medium-high. Coat 3 boneless skinless chicken breasts with 2 tbsp (30 mL) olive oil. Season with salt and pepper. Grill chicken, turning once, until no longer pink inside, 6 to 8 minutes per side. Transfer chicken to a cutting board. Let stand for 6 to 8 minutes. Slice into strips. Place on top of salad.

Sassy Southwest Salad

**Makes 4 to
6 servings**

This nutritious salad
is full of leafy romaine
lettuce. The jicama and
artichokes add texture
while the spicy brown
mustard and green chile
lace this salad with
flavor.

6 cups	chopped romaine lettuce	1.5 L
1	can (14 oz/398 mL) water-packed artichoke hearts, drained and quartered	1
1 cup	thin strips peeled jicama	250 mL

Dressing

⅓ cup	minced onion	75 mL
¾ cup	olive oil	175 mL
3 tbsp	apple cider vinegar	45 mL
½ tsp	granulated sugar	2 mL
½ tsp	salt	2 mL
Pinch	freshly ground black pepper	Pinch
2 tbsp	spicy brown mustard	30 mL
¼ cup	roasted green chile peppers, minced (see page 98)	60 mL
1 cup	corn tortillas, broken into bite-size pieces	250 mL
½ cup	crumbled Cotija cheese	125 mL

1. In a large bowl, gently toss together lettuce, artichoke hearts and jicama. Cover and refrigerate until chilled, for at least 30 minutes or for up to 4 hours.

2. *Dressing:* In a small bowl, whisk together onion, oil, vinegar, sugar, salt and pepper. Add mustard and green chiles. Whisk until well blended.

3. Pour dressing over lettuce mixture and toss to coat. Top with tortilla chips and cheese. Serve immediately.

Salpicon Beef Salad

Makes 6 servings

Salpicon is a term borrowed from the French, meaning a dish prepared with many diced and minced ingredients bound together by a sauce. This is a popular salad full of tender beef and fresh vegetables, and is typically served during the warmest months of the year along the border.

Variation

For a spicy flavor, in Step 2, add 1 cup (250 mL) chopped roasted New Mexico chiles (page 98).

3 lbs	beef brisket	1.5 kg
1	onion, quartered	1
2	cloves garlic	2
1 cup	Italian dressing	250 mL
3	chipotle chile peppers in adobo sauce, puréed	3
1 tbsp	finely chopped cilantro	15 mL
	Juice of 2 limes	
1 cup	shredded Monterey Jack cheese	250 mL
4	tomatoes, seeded and chopped	4
4	avocados	4
8	radishes, thinly sliced	8
	Flour or corn tortillas, warmed	

Garnishes, optional
Shredded lettuce
Diced tomato
Minced cilantro

1. In a large pot, place brisket, onion and garlic, adding enough water to cover by 1 inch (2.5 cm). Bring to a boil over medium-high heat. Reduce heat to low, cover and simmer until meat is tender and can be pulled apart easily, about 4 hours. Check and add more water if needed.

2. Remove meat from liquid and place on a cutting board. Discard liquid, onion and garlic. Let cool slightly. Using two forks shred thoroughly. Set aside.

3. In a large bowl, whisk together dressing, chipotle chiles, cilantro and 1 tbsp (15 mL) lime juice until well blended. Add meat and mix well. Add cheese and tomatoes and gently toss until well coated.

4. Transfer to a large serving bowl. Cover and refrigerate for at least 2 hours or for up to 6 hours to allow flavors to mingle.

5. Before serving, cut avocados lengthwise into thin slices. Place avocado on top of salad, arranging attractively, then place radish slices around edge of bowl. Serve with warm tortillas and additional garnish such as shredded lettuce, diced tomato and/or minced cilantro, if desired.

Spicy Tex-Mex Taco Salad

Makes 4 servings		

"Tex-Mex," the Texas version of Mexican cuisine, is popular around the world. This salad is no exception. The traditional recipe started with a ground beef filling, which I love. However, I have added a vegetarian version as well.

1 lb	ground beef, preferably sirloin	500 g
1	package (1.5 oz/45 g) taco seasoning	1
6 cups	chopped romaine lettuce	1.5 L
3 to 4 cups	crispy tortilla chips	750 mL to 1 L
1½ cups	shredded Cheddar cheese	375 mL
4	green onions, green parts only, chopped	4
2	tomatoes, seeded and diced	2
1 cup	sour cream	250 mL
½ cup	sliced black olives	125 mL

1. In a large skillet over medium heat, cook beef with the taco seasoning, and water recommended on the package, breaking up meat with a spoon, until meat is browned and no longer pink, about 12 minutes or as directed on the taco seasoning package. Set aside.

2. Divide lettuce equally among serving plates. Top with tortilla chips and meat mixture. Layer each salad with cheese, green onions, tomatoes, sour cream and black olives.

Variations

For more flavor, add ¼ cup (60 mL) diced avocado to each salad.

For a vegetarian salad, substitute 2 cups (500 mL) cooked or canned warm kidney beans, for the beef and omit the taco seasoning. Divide equally among salads.

Fresh Fajita Salad

Makes 4 servings

Some say fajitas originated back in the 1940s in West Texas where Mexican ranch hands cooked thin strips of meat and served them in a folded tortilla. Skirt steak accents this salad with flavor that makes for a light but hearty entrée.

6 cups	chopped romaine lettuce	1.5 L
1	onion, thinly sliced	1
1	red bell pepper, thinly sliced	1
1 cup	shredded Monterey Jack cheese	250 mL
1½ lbs	beef skirt steak, cut into ¼-inch (1 cm) strips	750 g
1 tbsp	olive oil	15 mL
1 tbsp	seasoned salt	15 mL
2	avocados	2
1 cup	sour cream	250 mL
1 cup	Pico de Gallo (page 56)	250 mL

1. In a large bowl, gently toss together lettuce, onion, bell pepper and cheese. Cover and refrigerate until chilled, for at least 30 minutes or for up to 4 hours.

2. In a medium bowl, toss steak strips in oil and season with salt.

3. In a large skillet, over high heat, sauté steak until edges are seared and centers are slightly pink, 4 to 6 minutes. Let steak stand for 6 to 8 minutes. Thinly slice meat across the grain, then into bite-size pieces.

4. Divide lettuce mixture among 4 plates. Dice avocados. Top each serving with equal amounts of grilled sirloin. Garnish with sour cream, avocados and Pico de Gallo.

> ### Variation
> Replace grilled sirloin with 1½ lbs (750 g) grilled chicken (page 148, Step 2).

Tacos, Tostadas, Burritos, Tortas and Tamales

continued...

Boneless Beef

Select a good cut of meat. Season lightly and slow-cook to create a perfect shredded beef filling. This recipe reflects on the traditional Mexican flavors of barbacoa. Customize this tender tasty meat for a variety of Mexican recipes.

Tip

The key to shredded beef is the meat should be falling apart and easy to shred. Measure out what you need for each recipe and freeze the remaining meat in an airtight container for up to 3 months.

2 to 3 lbs	boneless beef, chuck or sirloin roast	1 to 1.5 kg
1	onion, quartered	1
3	cloves garlic	3
¾ tsp	salt	3 mL

1. Place roast in a large pot and fill with enough water to cover the meat by 2 inches (5 cm). Add onion and garlic and bring to a gentle boil over medium-high heat. Cover, reduce heat to medium-low and simmer until meat is tender and falling apart, 1½ to 2 hours. Remove meat. Discard broth or use in another recipe. Let meat cool for 12 to 15 minutes. Shred meat into strands with your fingers or two forks. Add salt and mix well. Let cool completely. Measure out amount needed for recipe and place remaining beef in a resealable plastic bag. Refrigerate for up to 2 days or freeze for up to 3 months.

Variation

Slow-Cooker Method: Add beef, onion, garlic and 1 cup (250 mL) water to slow cooker stoneware. Slow cook on High for 4 to 5 hours. Strain, reserving broth and discarding onion and garlic. Shred meat into strands with your fingers or two forks. Let cool completely. Measure amount needed for taco, burrito or enchilada recipes.

Classic Rolled Tacos

From time to time, my girlfriends and I get together for taco-rolling parties. We make lots of tacos for the winter months ahead. They are simple and economical. I like to pack 12 uncooked tacos in a quart-size resealable plastic bag and place it in the freezer for up to 3 months. When you are ready to eat, thaw and fry as directed.

Tips

You do not need to seal the ends. The taco looks like a small flute.

Do not overcook these tacos, crispy on the ends and soft in the middle is a perfect rolled taco.

I recommend these sauces and salsas: Fiesta Taco Sauce (page 66) and Salsa Verde (page 58).

● Candy/deep-fry thermometer

2 cups	shredded cooked beef (see page 115 and Tips, page 117)	500 mL
¾ tsp	salt	3 mL
24	6-inch (15 cm) corn tortillas, micro-warmed (page 74)	24
	Vegetable oil	

1. In a large bowl, thoroughly combine shredded beef and salt.

2. To build tacos, place about $1\frac{1}{2}$ tbsp (22 mL) of meat at one end of each tortilla, shaping the filling into a short, straight line. Gently roll tortilla and secure with a toothpick (see Tips, left). Deep-fry immediately or place rolled tacos in a resealable plastic bag to keep moist. Refrigerate until ready to cook for up to 2 days.

3. Fill a deep fryer, deep heavy pot or deep skillet with 3 inches (7.5 cm) of oil and heat to 350°F (180°C). Using tongs, gently place 3 to 4 tacos at a time in the hot oil and deep-fry, turning once, until golden brown and crispy, 2 to 3 minutes. Drain on paper towels. Lightly season with salt. Serve 3 or 4 per person.

Variation

You could substitute 2 cups (500 mL) cooked and crumbled ground beef for the taco filling.

Traditional Folded Tacos

Makes 8 tacos

True, authentic folded tacos start with a good shredded beef filling and crispy taco shells. I slow cook a roast, season and shred it. Make ahead and freeze for convenience.

Tips

Follow directions on page 115 for shredded cooked beef or use any leftover cooked roast or steak, shredded by hand or with two forks.

If you are short on time, use store-bought taco shells. There are a variety of brands to choose from. Check with your local grocer to see if they make them fresh.

2 cups	shredded cooked beef see page 115 and Tips, left)	500 mL
	Salt and freshly ground black pepper	
8	taco shells (see Tips, left and page 118)	8
1½ cups	shredded lettuce	375 mL
1 cup	shredded Cheddar cheese	250 mL
1	onion, minced	1
1	tomato, seeded and diced	1

1. In a large bowl, toss meat with salt and pepper to taste.

2. To build tacos, divide meat equally among taco shells, gently placing meat in the shells. Top meat with lettuce, cheese and onion. Garnish with tomato chunks.

Variations

Substitute shredded beef with 1 lb (500 g) ground beef, preferably sirloin, cooked until meat is browned and no longer pink, about 12 minutes. Drain off excess fat. Season with salt and pepper.

For chicken tacos, substitute 2 cups (500 mL) shredded cooked chicken for beef. Season with salt and pepper.

To heighten the flavor, use a variety of lettuce greens and Mexican cheeses (page 25).

Folded Taco Shells

||||||||||||||||||||||||||||||||||||||||||||||||||||||||||||||||||||||||||||||||||||||||||||||

Makes 8 taco shells

I like to make my own taco shells. They have a light crispy texture. They won't crumble and fall apart, making them easy to stuff with filling. The secret to making the perfect shape is to make a foil mold, which helps keep the tortilla wide enough to insert your delicious fillings.

||||||||||||||||||||||||||||||||||||||||||||||||

Tips

Kitchen gloves or grilling mitts are heat resistant, with a long form-fitting cuff that gives you protection when grilling or deep-frying. You can find these online or in most kitchen supply stores.

Peanut oil has a higher smoke point than other oils. It tends to crisp tortillas faster and help them retain less oil.

- Heavy-duty foil
- Kitchen gloves (see Tips, left)
- Candy/deep-fry thermometer

8	corn or flour tortillas (pages 70 to 73)	8
	Peanut oil (see Tips, left)	

1. Cut a 4-foot by 12-inch (120 by 30 cm) piece of foil. Fold it in half so you have a 2-foot (60 cm) long piece. Fold edges in toward the center 2 inches (5 cm) on each side. You will have a 2-foot by 8-inch (60 by 20 cm) piece of foil. Fold each end toward the middle every 4 inches (10 cm) three times until both ends meet in the middle. Shape into a narrow "U" shape. This creates a mold that you can wrap your tortilla around.

2. In a deep fryer or deep heavy pot, heat 3 inches (7.5 cm) of oil to 350°F (180°C). Working with one tortilla at a time, wrap tortilla around foil mold to make the taco shape, holding it at the top of the mold with your thumb and index finger or tongs. Dip center of tortilla (wrapped around the mold) into oil and fry for about 2 minutes until center is crispy and hard. Using tongs, carefully remove foil mold and place on a paper towel. Holding the shell with tongs, immerse one side of the taco shell in oil and fry until crisp and golden brown. Repeat with second side of tortilla, creating a "U" shaped shell. Transfer to a paper towel-lined surface to drain. Adjust heat as necessary between taco shells.

Flautas

Makes 12 tacos

Flauta, **Spanish for flute, is a Sonoran-style taco authentic to the northwestern part of Mexico and also popular in many parts of Arizona. A flour tortilla creates a lighter, flakier, crust-like shell for your "rolled" taco. The key is to find small flour tortillas, then stuff them with this tasty meat filling.**

Tips

Small flour tortillas are hard to find. You can make your own (pages 72 and 73). If you are using store-bought tortillas, look for the smallest, usually 8-inch (20 cm), and trim to a 6-inch (15 cm) size with a pair of kitchen shears.

Follow directions on page 115 for shredded cooked beef or use any leftover cooked roast or steak, shredded by hand or with two forks.

- Candy/deep-fry thermometer

2 cups	shredded cooked beef (see page 115 and Tips, left)	500 mL
¾ tsp	salt	3 mL
12	6-inch (15 cm) flour tortillas, micro- or skillet-warmed (pages 74 and 75)	12
	Vegetable oil	

1. In a large bowl, thoroughly combine shredded meat and salt.

2. To build tacos, divide meat equally among tortillas and place at one end of each tortilla. Gently roll tortilla and secure with a toothpick (see Tips, page 116). Deep-fry immediately or place rolled tacos in a resealable plastic bag to keep moist. Refrigerate until ready to cook for up to 2 days.

3. Fill a deep fryer, deep heavy pot or deep skillet with 3 inches (7.5 cm) of oil and heat to 350°F (180°C). Using tongs, gently place 4 tacos at a time in the hot oil and deep-fry, turning once, until crispy and golden brown, about 2 minutes. Drain on paper towels. Lightly season with salt.

Variation

Substitute 2 cups (500 mL) shredded cooked chicken for the beef and add salt. Continue with Step 2.

Sonoran Bean and Cheese Tacos

Makes 16 rolled tacos		

This light, flaky crisp taco is a favorite among kids. Creating a rolled taco with a fried flour tortilla is a mainstay in Sonoran-style cooking. Also known as a *flauta*, these vegetarian tacos are delicious.

Tip

Serve with Fiesta Taco Sauce (page 66), Green Chile and Jalapeño Salsa (page 58) or Salsa Verde (page 58).

• Candy/deep-fry thermometer

2 cups	Quick Refried Beans or Stove Top Refried Beans (page 100)	500 mL
16	6-inch (15 cm) flour tortillas, micro- or skillet-warmed (pages 74 and 75)	16
1 cup	shredded Monterey Jack cheese	250 mL
	Vegetable oil	
	Salt	

1. To build tacos, place 2 tbsp (30 mL) of the beans at one end of each tortilla, shaping the filling into a short, straight line. Top with equal amounts of cheese. Gently roll tortilla and secure with a toothpick. Repeat with remaining tortillas. Deep-fry immediately or place rolled tacos in a resealable plastic bag to keep moist. Refrigerate until ready to cook for up to 2 days or place in freezer for up to 4 months. Thaw completely before cooking.

2. Fill deep fryer, deep heavy pot or deep skillet with 3 inches (7.5 cm) of oil and heat to 350°F (180°C). Using tongs, gently place 4 to 6 tacos at a time in the hot oil and deep-fry until crispy and golden brown, about 2 minutes. Drain on paper towels. Lightly season with salt.

Crispy Potato Tacos

Makes 8 tacos

Perfect for a Sunday brunch or lazy morning breakfast. Baked potato accented with a bit of bacon is the perfect combination for these tacos.

- Preheat oven to 350°F (180°C)
- Candy/deep-fry thermometer

2	baking potatoes	2
4	slices bacon, cooked and crumbled	4
8	6- to 8-inch (15 to 20 cm) corn tortillas, micro-warmed (page 74)	8
	Vegetable oil	

1. Place potatoes on a baking sheet. Bake in preheated oven until tender throughout, about 1 hour. Let cool. Leave skins on, dice and mash slightly.

2. In a large bowl, combine potatoes and bacon.

3. To build tacos, divide potato mixture equally among tortillas, placing mixture on one half of tortilla. Fold over and secure edges with several toothpicks. Deep-fry immediately or place folded tacos in a resealable plastic bag to keep moist. Refrigerate until ready to cook for up to 2 days.

4. Fill a deep fryer, deep heavy pot or deep skillet with 3 inches (7.5 cm) of oil and heat to 350°F (180°C). Using tongs, gently place 2 to 3 tacos at a time into the hot oil and deep-fry, turning once, until golden brown and crispy, 2 to 3 minutes. Drain on paper towels. Serve hot.

Variation

Serve with Roasted Tomato Salsa (page 56) or Green Chile and Jalapeño Salsa (page 58).

Crispy Potato Taquitos

Makes 16 tacos	

Tasty little tacos served on a platter covered in cabbage and Mexican cheese make a great snack or entrée.

Tips

Wash and cut 2 medium potatoes into $\frac{1}{4}$-inch (0.5 cm) cubes. Fill a large pot half full of water. Bring water to a boil over high heat. Add potatoes and boil until soft, about 15 minutes. Drain and cool completely.

You can also bake 2 medium-size potatoes for $1\frac{1}{2}$ hours in a preheated 350°F (180°C) oven until tender throughout. Let cool and then dice.

You do not need to seal the ends. The taco looks like a small flute.

● Candy/deep-fry thermometer

$2\frac{1}{2}$ cups	diced cooked potatoes, slightly mashed (see Tips, left)	625 mL
16	6-inch (15 cm) corn tortillas, micro-warmed (page 74)	16
	Vegetable oil	
	Salt	
2 cups	shredded cabbage	500 mL
1 cup	crumbled Cotija cheese (see Tips, page 108)	250 mL

1. To build tacos, place 2 heaping tbsp (30 mL) of the potatoes at one end of each tortilla, shaping the filling into a short, straight line. Gently roll tortilla and secure with a toothpick. Deep-fry immediately or place taquitos in a resealable plastic bag to keep moist. Refrigerate until ready to cook for up to 2 days.

2. Fill deep fryer, deep heavy pot or deep skillet with 3 inches (7.5 cm) of oil and heat to 350°F (180°C). Using tongs, gently place 3 to 4 taquitos at a time in the hot oil and deep-fry, turning once, until golden brown and crispy, 2 to 3 minutes. Drain on paper towels. Lightly season with salt.

3. To serve, place 3 to 4 taquitos on a plate. Top with equal amounts of cabbage and cheese. Serve with a favorite salsa or taco sauce.

Pollo Verde Tacos

	Makes 8 tacos	

These tacos include a stew-like chicken filling smothered in a green chile sauce. So quick to make, this taco is perfect for last-minute entertaining or a late-night meal.

Tip

When I am pressed for time I pick up a roasted chicken from the deli section of my grocery store. Typically one 4-lb (2 kg) roasted cooked chicken will yield approximately 4 cups (1 L) of cooked diced chicken.

2 tbsp	olive oil, divided	30 mL
2	cloves garlic, minced	2
1	onion, diced	1
½ cup	chopped roasted New Mexico or Anaheim green chile peppers (2 to 3, depending on size) (see page 98)	125 mL
1½ lbs	boneless skinless chicken breasts, cut into ¼-inch (0.5 cm) cubes	750 g
8	6- to 8-inch (15 to 20 cm) corn tortillas, skillet-warmed (page 74)	8
1 cup	shredded Monterey Jack cheese	250 mL
2 cups	chopped salad mix	500 mL

1. In a large skillet, heat 1 tbsp (15 mL) of the oil over medium-high heat. Sauté garlic until tender, about 1 minute. Add onion and chiles and sauté until onions are transparent, 4 to 6 minutes. Set aside.

2. In same skillet over medium-high heat, add remaining 1 tbsp (15 mL) of oil. Sauté chicken until no longer pink inside and juices have evaporated, 10 to 12 minutes. Return onion mixture to skillet and sauté until hot, 3 to 4 minutes.

3. To build tacos, divide chicken mixture equally among tortillas. Top with cheese and salad mix. Fold tortillas in half.

Tacos el Pastor

	Makes 8 tacos	

These pineapple and pork tacos are the original fusion food — a cross between Middle Eastern shawarma and Mexican chile-rubbed grilled pork. This is my version of Mexico's favorite taco.

Tip

Serve with bowls of fresh cilantro leaves, chopped radishes, crumbled Cotija cheese or queso fresco cheese, chopped onions and jalapeños.

- Blender or food processor

½ cup	canned pineapple chunks, juice reserved	125 mL
1	onion, chopped	1
2 tbsp	minced cilantro	30 mL
5	chipotle chile peppers in adobo sauce	5
1½ lbs	pork tenderloin, cut into ½-inch (1 cm) cubes	750 g
1 tbsp	olive oil	15 mL
16	6-inch (15 cm) corn tortillas	16
	Pico de Gallo (page 56)	
4	limes, cut into wedges	4

1. In blender or food processor, purée pineapple, onion, cilantro and chiles until smooth. Add a bit of pineapple juice if the purée is too thick.

2. In a resealable plastic bag, combine pork and pineapple marinade and seal bag. Refrigerate for at least 4 hours or for up to 24 hours.

3. Remove pork from marinade, discarding marinade. In a large skillet, heat oil over medium-high heat. Sauté pork until browned and cooked through, about 10 minutes.

4. To build tacos, skillet warm tortillas (page 74). Stack 2 tortillas per taco, divide pork among tortillas. Top with Pico de Gallo. Fold tortillas in half. Serve each with a lime wedge.

Grilled Carne Asada Tacos

Makes 12 tacos		

Carne Asada is an intensely flavored meat that is very popular in Mexico. It is quick to marinate and easy to grill.

Tip

There are several different cuts of meat you can use for this recipe. Skirt steak or minute steak are best due to the thin cut and quick cooking time.

● Barbecue grill

Marinade

	Juice of 3 lemons	
3	cloves garlic, minced	3
½ cup	drained sliced pickled jalapeño peppers	125 mL
½ cup	teriyaki sauce	125 mL
1 tbsp	minced red bell pepper	15 mL
1 tbsp	granulated sugar	15 mL
2 tsp	kosher salt	10 mL
1½ lbs	beef skirt or minute steak (see Tip, left)	750 g
12	6- to 8-inch (15 to 20 cm) flour or corn tortillas	12
	Pico de Gallo (page 56)	
2	limes, each cut into 6 wedges	2

1. *Marinade:* In a medium bowl, combine lemon juice, garlic, jalapeños, teriyaki sauce, bell pepper, sugar and salt until sugar and salt have dissolved.

2. In a large resealable plastic bag, add marinade and meat and seal. Work marinade through meat with your fingers. Refrigerate meat for at least 2 hours or for up to 6 hours.

3. Preheat greased barbecue grill to medium. Remove meat from marinade, discarding marinade. Grill meat for 4 to 5 minutes per side for medium-rare. Remove from grill and let stand for 8 to 10 minutes. Carve meat across the grain into thin slices, then cut into bite-size pieces.

4. To build tacos, skillet warm tortillas (page 75). Divide meat equally among tortillas and top with Pico de Gallo. Fold tortillas in half. Serve with a sliced lime.

Pollo Asada Tacos

Makes 12 tacos

This intensely flavored marinade delivers flavor and texture. Chicken breasts are quick to marinate and easy to grill.

Tip

If you are pressed for time, omit the bell pepper, garlic, sugar and salt. In a small bowl, combine 1 package (0.7 oz/19 g) dry Italian dressing mix with lemon juice, jalapeños and teriyaki sauce. Continue with Step 2.

● Barbecue grill

	Juice of 3 lemons	
3	cloves garlic, minced	3
½ cup	drained sliced pickled jalapeño peppers	125 mL
½ cup	teriyaki sauce	125 mL
1 tbsp	minced red bell pepper	15 mL
1 tbsp	granulated sugar	15 mL
1 tsp	kosher salt	5 mL
2 lbs	boneless skinless chicken breasts	1 kg
12	6-inch (15 cm) corn tortillas	12
	Green Chile and Jalapeño Salsa (page 58)	

1. In a medium bowl, combine lemon juice, garlic, jalapeños, teriyaki sauce, bell pepper, sugar and salt, mixing until sugar and salt are dissolved.

2. In a large resealable plastic bag, combine marinade and chicken. Seal bag and work marinade into chicken with your fingers. Refrigerate for at least 2 hours or for up to 6 hours.

3. Preheat greased grill to medium-high heat. Remove chicken from marinade, discarding marinade. Grill chicken, turning once, until no longer pink inside, 6 to 8 minutes per side. Transfer chicken to a cutting board and let stand for 6 to 8 minutes. Cut into thin slices.

4. To build tacos, skillet warm tortillas (page 74). Divide chicken equally among tortillas. Top with salsa. Fold tortillas in half. Serve each with a lime wedge.

> ## Variation
>
> For a richer flavor, top each taco with 1 tbsp (15 mL) Fiesta Guacamole (page 51).

Beef Carnita Tacos

Makes 12 tacos		
1 tbsp	olive oil	15 mL
1½ lbs	boneless beef sirloin steak, cut into bite-size pieces	750 g
1½ tsp	seasoned salt	7 mL
½ tsp	garlic powder	2 mL
12	6- to 8-inch (15 to 20 cm) corn or flour tortillas, skillet-warmed (pages 74 and 75)	12
2	limes, each cut into 6 wedges	2
	Charred Corn Guacamole (page 52)	
	Pico de Gallo (page 56)	

Tender, seared meats are a Mexican favorite when it comes to beefy tacos. Simple flavors topped with fresh Guacamole and Pico de Gallo make a celebration favorite.

1. In a large skillet, heat oil over high heat. Add meat, seasoned salt and garlic powder, stirring, until meat is slightly charred and slightly pink inside.

2. To build tacos, divide meat equally among tortillas. Top with guacamole and Pico de Gallo.

Variation

You can serve this taco with bowls of a variety of additional fresh toppings, such as diced tomato, minced green onion, shredded lettuce and fresh cilantro.

Classic Carnita Tacos with Fresh Lime

Makes 16 tacos

This shredded pork taco is a timeless classic in Mexico. My recipe ties together the distinctive flavors of Mexico — chile, pork and lime. Tacos make great party food and these are no exception.

2 lb	boneless pork shoulder blade (butt) roast, cubed	1 kg
1	onion, sliced	1
2	cloves garlic, chopped	2
2 tbsp	kosher salt	30 mL
1 tbsp	olive oil	15 mL
2	onions, diced	2
4	serrano chile or jalapeño peppers, seeded and chopped	4
16	6- to 8-inch (15 to 20 cm) corn tortillas	16
4	limes, cut into quarter wedges	4

1. Place pork in a large pot. Add just enough water to cover. Add sliced onion, garlic and salt and bring to a boil over medium-high heat. Reduce heat to medium-low, cover and boil gently until pork is tender, 2 to 3 hours. Remove pork from pot, reserving 1 cup (250 mL) of liquid. Let pork cool slightly, then shred or chop into tiny pieces, discarding excess fat.

2. In a large skillet, heat oil over medium heat. Add diced onions and chiles and cook, stirring, until tender, 4 to 6 minutes. Add pork and reserved liquid. Cook over medium-high heat, stirring, until all juices have evaporated, about 15 minutes.

Tip

Serve with bowls of fresh cilantro leaves, chopped radishes, crumbled Cotija cheese or queso fresco cheese, chopped onions and jalapeños.

3. To build tacos, skillet warm tortillas (page 74). Divide pork mixture equally among tortillas. Fold tortillas in half. Serve each with a fresh lime wedge.

Variations

Red Chile Carnitas: Add 1½ cups (375 mL) Red Enchilada Sauce (page 63) or store-bought red enchilada sauce in Step 2 after juices have evaporated. Cook over medium heat until heated through, 6 to 8 minutes.

Red Chile Carnitas with Hominy: Increase tortillas to 24. Add 1½ cups (375 mL) Red Enchilada Sauce (page 63) or store-bought red enchilada sauce and 1 cup (250 mL) drained minced hominy in Step 2 after juices have evaporated. Cook, stirring, over medium heat until heated through, 6 to 8 minutes.

Grilled Mahi Mahi Tacos

Makes 8 tacos

This lightly seasoned fillet can be grilled or sautéed to create the perfect filling for a taco. Layering cream sauce and salsa boosts the texture and flavor.

1½ lbs	mahi mahi fillets	750 g
2 tbsp	olive oil	30 mL
¾ tsp	salt	3 mL
½ tsp	freshly ground black pepper	2 mL
8	6-inch (15 cm) corn tortillas, skillet-warmed (page 74)	8
	Basic Taco Cream Sauce (page 67)	
2 cups	shredded cabbage	500 mL
	Citrus Salsa (page 59)	

1. Rinse mahi mahi and pat dry with paper towel. Brush fillets with oil on both sides. Season with salt and pepper. Grill fillets, turning once, until opaque in center, 3 to 4 minutes per side. Transfer to a cutting board and cut into bite-size pieces.

2. To build tacos, divide fish equally among tortillas. Top with Basic Taco Cream Sauce, cabbage and Citrus Salsa. Fold tortillas in half.

Variations

Serve each taco with 1 tbsp (15 mL) Classic Guacamole (page 51).

Divide ¼ cup (60 mL) minced pickled jalapeños equally among tacos.

Halibut Tacos

Makes 8 tacos

Simply grilled halibut defines this taco. Cool fresh flavors are added with avocado, tomato and lime.

• Preheat greased barbecue grill to medium-high heat

1½ lbs	halibut steaks	750 g
2 tbsp	olive oil	30 mL
1 tsp	salt	5 mL
½ tsp	freshly ground black pepper	2 mL
8	6- to 8-inch (15 to 20 cm) flour tortillas, skillet-warmed (page 75)	8
1	tomato, seeded and diced	1
2	avocados, diced	2
2	limes, each cut into 4 wedges	2

1. Rinse halibut and pat dry with paper towel. Brush steaks with oil on both sides. Season with salt and pepper. Grill halibut, turning once, until firm and opaque in the center, about 4 minutes per side. Transfer fish to cutting board and cut into bite-size pieces.

2. To build tacos, divide fish equally among tortillas. Top with tomato and avocados. Fold tortillas in half. Serve with a wedge of lime.

Variation

Add 8 oz (250 g) spicy Cajun sausage to the halibut in Step 1. Grill sausage over medium heat, turning often, until lightly browned and juices run clear, 6 to 8 minutes per side. Transfer sausage to cutting board and cut into bite-size pieces. Divide equally among tortillas.

Fresh Baja Fish Tacos

Makes 8 tacos		

Baja, the peninsula of Mexico located south of California, is famous for its fish tacos. Fish tacos are gaining popularity around the globe. These lightly fried fish delights are layered with cabbage, cream sauce and Pico de Gallo.

Mexican White Sauce

¾ cup	mayonnaise	175 mL
½ cup	plain yogurt	125 mL
	Juice of 1 lime	
1 cup	all-purpose flour	250 mL
¾ cup	light beer	175 mL
1 tsp	kosher salt	5 mL
1½ lbs	skinless cod or tilapia fillets (see Tip, right)	750 g
	Vegetable oil	
8	6- to 8-inch (15 to 20 cm) corn or flour tortillas	8
1 cup	thinly shredded red cabbage	250 mL
1 cup	thinly shredded green cabbage	250 mL
	Pico de Gallo (page 56)	

1. *Mexican White Sauce:* In a small bowl, combine mayonnaise, yogurt and lime juice. Cover and refrigerate for at least 2 hours or for up to 24 hours.

2. In a large bowl, combine flour, beer and salt. Mix well to a thick consistency.

3. Rinse fish and pat dry with paper towel. Cut crosswise into 1-inch (2.5 cm) wide strips.

4. Fill a deep fryer, deep heavy pot or deep skillet with 1 inch (2.5 cm) of oil and heat to 350°F (180°C). Using tongs, dredge fish pieces in batter and gently place in oil. Deep-fry 3 to 4 pieces at a time, turning once, until golden brown, about 1 minute per side. Drain on paper towels. Discard any excess batter.

There are concerns about the sustainability of some fish and seafood, so we recommend you check reliable sites such as www.seachoice.org for the latest information.

5. To build tacos, skillet warm tortillas (page 74). Divide fish equally among tortillas. Top with cabbage, Mexican White Sauce and Pico de Gallo. Fold tortillas in half.

Variation

For added flavor, add a pinch each of ground cumin, dried oregano and ground white pepper to the Basic Taco Cream Sauce (page 67).

Grilled Spicy Shrimp Tacos

Makes 8 tacos

Lightly grilled shrimp glazed with chipotle chile has a smooth, distinctive taste — smoky and rich. I love this shrimp filling topped with a sweet yet fiery corn salsa.

Tip

Flat skewers work best so shrimp does not flip around while turning. You can also thread shrimp on two skewers parallel to each other.

- Preheat greased barbecue grill to medium-high
- 4 wooden skewers, soaked in water for 30 minutes (see Tip, left)

4	chipotle chile peppers in adobo sauce, puréed	4
¼ cup	liquid honey	60 mL
2 tbsp	olive oil	30 mL
16 to 24	medium shrimp, peeled and deveined (see Tip, left)	16 to 24
8	6-inch (15 cm) corn tortillas, skillet-warmed (page 74)	8
2 cups	shredded cabbage	500 mL
	Fiery Corn Salsa (page 59)	

1. In a medium bowl, combine chipotle purée, honey and oil.

2. Thread 4 to 6 shrimp on each skewer. Grill, turning once, until shrimp turns pink, 3 to 4 minutes per side. Brush shrimp with chile glaze and grill, turning once, until shrimp are opaque throughout, for 1 minute more per side. Transfer to a platter.

3. To build tacos, divide shrimp equally among tortillas. Top with cabbage and Fiery Corn Salsa. Fold tortillas in half.

Chorizo, Egg and Potato Tacos

| Makes 8 tacos | |

This breakfast combination is an all-time favorite in the Southwest. The chorizo, a spicy Mexican sausage, and crispy potato are perfect together, nestled among the fluffy scrambled eggs.

Tips

Top this taco with Roasted Tomato Salsa (page 56) or Salsa Verde (page 58).

I like this breakfast taco because it takes very little time to prepare and all 8 tacos can be made ahead and kept warm, covered, in a preheated 200°F (100°C) oven for up to 1 hour.

1 tbsp	olive oil	15 mL
1	potato, cut into 1/4-inch (0.5 cm) dice	1
	Salt	
4 oz	fresh chorizo sausage, removed from casings	125 g
4	eggs, lightly beaten	4
8	6-inch (15 cm) corn tortillas, skillet-warmed (page 74)	8
1 cup	shredded Cheddar cheese	250 mL

1. In a medium skillet, heat oil over medium heat. Add potato and cook, covered, about 10 minutes. Remove lid, and cook, stirring, until potato is soft, lightly browned and crispy, 8 to 10 minutes more. Season with salt to taste.

2. Reduce heat to medium-low. Add chorizo to potato in skillet and fry chorizo, breaking up with a spoon until well browned, 8 to 10 minutes. Drain excess grease. Add eggs and cook, stirring, until set.

3. To build tacos, divide egg mixture equally among tortillas. Top with cheese. Fold tortillas in half.

Bean and Cheese Chimichangas

**Makes
4 chimichangas**

Chimichangas consist of delicious fillings wrapped in a flour tortilla, deep-fried until golden brown and smothered in a mild enchilada sauce and melted cheese. However, many people like chimichangas with no sauce, enjoying them as a "hand-held" chimichanga.

Tip

Make sure all ends are sealed so filling does not escape while frying.

● Candy/deep-fry thermometer

2 cups	Quick Refried Beans or Stove Top Refried Beans (page 100)	500 mL
4	10-inch (25 cm) flour tortillas, micro- or skillet-warmed (pages 74 and 75)	4
1 cup	shredded Monterey Jack cheese	250 mL
	Vegetable oil	
	Salt	

1. To build chimichangas, place $\frac{1}{2}$ cup (125 mL) of the beans on bottom half of each tortilla. Sprinkle with cheese, dividing equally. Fold bottom edge of tortilla up over the beans. Fold in both sides of tortilla. Starting at folded bottom edge, roll up to enclose filling. Secure with a toothpick. Place chimichangas in a resealable plastic bag to keep moist. Refrigerate for at least 1 hour to firm up filling or for up to 4 hours.

2. Fill deep fryer, deep heavy pot or deep skillet with 3 inches (7.5 cm) of oil and heat to 350°F (180°C). Using tongs, gently place 1 to 2 chimichangas at a time in the hot oil and deep-fry, turning once, until crispy and golden brown, 2 to 4 minutes. Drain on paper towels. Lightly season with salt. Serve hot.

Shredded Beef Chimichangas

Makes
4 chimichangas

Crispy flour tortilla filled with tender shredded beef makes a chimichanga you won't forget. These can be made ahead and placed in the freezer for up to 3 months for last-minute entertaining.

Tips

Make sure all ends are sealed so filling does not escape while frying.

If you want to prepare chimichangas ahead and freeze, place them in a resealable plastic bag and freeze for up to 3 months. Thaw at room temperature and serve with suggested sauces.

- Candy/deep-fry thermometer
- Preheat oven to 350°F (180°C)
- Ovenproof plates

2 cups	shredded cooked beef (see page 115)	500 mL
	Salt and freshly ground black pepper	
4	10-inch (25 mL) flour tortillas	4
	Vegetable oil	
1 cup	shredded Monterey Jack cheese	250 mL
2 cups	Green Enchilada Sauce (page 64) or Red Enchilada Sauce (page 63), warmed	500 mL

1. In a large bowl, toss meat with salt and pepper to taste.

2. To build chimichangas, divide meat mixture equally among tortillas, placing on bottom edge. Fold bottom edge of tortilla up over filling. Fold in both sides of the tortilla. Starting at folded bottom edge, roll up to enclose filling. Secure with a toothpick.

3. Fill deep fryer, deep heavy pot or deep skillet with 3 inches (7.5 cm) of oil and heat to 350°F (180°C). Using tongs, gently place 1 to 2 chimichangas at a time in the hot oil and deep-fry, turning once, until crispy and golden brown, about 2 minutes per side. Drain on paper towels. Lightly season with salt.

4. Place chimichangas on individual plates. Divide sauce and cheese among chimichangas. Bake in preheated oven until cheese is melted and bubbly, 12 to 15 minutes.

Chile Relleno Tacos

Makes 8 tacos

Although chile rellenos are a lot of work, they are well worth it if you have the time. Here is a quick rendition of a wonderful Mexican treasure, an egg-battered tortilla stuffed with chile and cheese.

Tip

This taco is so versatile. Serve them for breakfast, lunch or dinner. I have even served them as a side dish along with grilled meats and salad.

2 cups	chopped roasted green chile peppers (see page 98)	500 mL
1 cup	shredded Cheddar cheese	250 mL
1 cup	shredded Monterey Jack cheese	250 mL
8	6- to 8-inch (15 to 20 cm) flour tortillas, micro-warmed (page 74)	8
8	eggs, lightly beaten	8
1 cup	all-purpose flour	250 mL

1. To build tacos, divide chiles and Cheddar and Monterey Jack cheeses equally among tortillas, placing on one half of the tortilla. Fold over and secure edges with toothpicks. Place filled tortillas in a large resealable plastic bag and refrigerate until ready to cook or for up to 8 hours.

2. Place eggs in a shallow dish. Place flour in another shallow dish. Dip each taco in the egg mixture quickly and then flour on both sides. Then dip into egg mixture again.

3. Spray a large skillet with cooking spray and heat over medium-high heat. Add egg-dipped tacos, in batches of 2 or 3, and toast until cheese is melted and tortilla is golden brown, 4 to 6 minutes per side.

Bean and Cheese Burritos

||||||||||||||||||||||||||||||||||||||||||||||||||||||||||||||||||||||||||||||||||||||||||||||||||||||||

Makes 4 burritos

Sometimes the simplest things are the most enjoyable. My kids grew up on bean and cheese burritos. Once in a while they would eat them with enchilada sauce but most of the time just tasty refried beans and cheese wrapped in a fresh flour tortilla.

|||||||||||||||||||||||||||||||||||||||||||||||

Tip

Refrigerate after Step 1 until ready to cook for up to 2 days or place in freezer in resealable plastic bags for up to 4 months. Thaw completely in the refrigerator before serving. Reheat as directed in Step 2.

- Preheat oven to 375°F (190°C)
- Ovenproof plates

2 cups	Quick Refried Beans or Stove Top Refried Beans (page 100)	500 mL
4	10-inch (25 cm) flour tortillas, micro- or skillet-warmed (pages 74 and 75)	4
2 cups	shredded Monterey Jack cheese, divided	500 mL
2 cups	Red Enchilada Sauce (page 63) or Green Enchilada Sauce (page 64), warmed	500 mL

1. To build burritos, spread $\frac{1}{2}$ cup (125 mL) of the beans on bottom half of each tortilla. Sprinkle with 1 cup (250 mL) of the cheese, dividing equally. Fold bottom edge of tortilla up over beans. Starting at folded bottom edge, roll up to enclose filling. Secure with a toothpick.

2. Place burritos seam side down on individual ovenproof plates. Divide sauce and remaining cheese equally among each burrito. Bake in preheated oven until warmed and cheese is melted, 12 to 15 minutes.

Machaca Burritos

Makes 4 burritos

This beefy filling is infused with citrus and chile flavor. The word *machaca* comes from the Spanish verb machacar, meaning to pound or crush. Culinary history tells us this meat was seasoned, cured and dried for many hours. Today, we can get the same taste by cooking in flavor and cooking out the juices. I like to serve enchilada-style with a light Sonoran sauce.

Tip

Machaca also goes well with both red and green enchilada sauces so occasionally I top my burritos with both. You will get an entirely different flavor by using Red Enchilada Sauce (page 63), which has a rich earthy flavor. However, Green Enchilada Sauce (page 64) adds a lighter, spicy flavor to this burrito. Sometimes I serve it with both, which I call Machaca Burrito de Christmas!

- Preheat oven to 375°F (190°C)
- Ovenproof plates

1 tbsp	vegetable oil	15 mL
2	cloves garlic, minced	2
1	onion, diced	1
½ cup	roasted green chile pepper (see page 98)	125 mL
1	tomato, seeded and chopped	1
2 cups	shredded cooked beef (see page 115)	500 mL
⅓ cup	beef broth	75 mL
	Juice of 2 limes	
	Salt and freshly ground black pepper	
4	10-inch (25 cm) flour tortillas, skillet-warmed (page 75)	4
1 cup	shredded Monterey Jack cheese	250 mL
	Sonoran Enchilada Sauce, warmed (page 65)	

1. In a large skillet, heat oil over medium-low heat. Add garlic, onion, chiles and tomato and cook, stirring, until onion is translucent, 8 to 10 minutes. Add beef, beef broth and lime juice. Increase heat to medium and cook, stirring, until all juices have evaporated, 12 to 15 minutes. Season with salt and pepper to taste.

2. To build burritos, divide meat mixture equally among tortillas, placing on bottom edge. Top with cheese. Fold bottom edge of tortilla up over filling. Starting at folded bottom edge, roll up to enclose filling. Secure with a toothpick.

3. Place burritos seam side down on individual ovenproof plates. Divide cheese and sauce equally among burritos. Place in preheated oven until cheese is melted and bubbly and burritos are heated through, 12 to 15 minutes.

Pollo Verde Burritos

Makes 4 burritos		

These burritos are so satisfying. Warm chicken wrapped in a tortilla with a little chile is the perfect meal on a busy weeknight.

- Preheated 375°F (190°C)
- Ovenproof plates

1 tbsp	olive oil	15 mL
1	clove garlic, minced	1
½ cup	roasted green chile peppers (see page 98)	125 mL
1	onion, diced	1
¼ cup	chicken broth	60 mL
2 cups	diced cooked chicken (see page 115)	500 mL
4	10-inch (25 cm) flour tortillas, skillet-warmed (page 75)	4
2 cups	Green Enchilada Sauce (page 64)	500 mL
½ cup	shredded Monterey Jack cheese	125 mL
½ cup	shredded Cheddar cheese	125 mL

1. In a large skillet, heat oil over medium heat. Add garlic and cook, stirring, until tender, about 1 minute. Add chiles and onion and cook, stirring, until onion is translucent, 4 to 6 minutes. Add broth and chicken and simmer, stirring occasionally, until chicken is heated through, 8 to 10 minutes.

2. To build burritos, divide meat mixture equally among tortillas, placing on bottom edge. Fold bottom edge of tortilla up over filling. Starting at folded bottom edge, roll up to enclose filling. Secure with a toothpick.

3. Place burritos seam side down on individual ovenproof plates. Divide sauce and cheese among burritos. Bake in preheated oven until cheese is melted and bubbly and burritos are heated through, 12 to 15 minutes.

Variation

If you enjoy more melted cheese in your burrito, add an extra ½ cup (125 mL) each Monterey Jack and Cheddar cheeses in Step 3.

Carne Adovada

Makes 4 cups (1 L)

This is a red chile pork filling in a thick red sauce that I use in a variety of Mexican dishes. It is perfect for tamales, burritos, burrito bowls and topping tostadas.

2 lb	boneless pork shoulder blade (butt), cut into bite-size pieces	1 kg
2 cups	Red Enchilada Sauce (page 63)	500 mL
1 tsp	hot pepper flakes	5 mL
1 tsp	dried oregano	5 mL
1 tsp	ground cumin	5 mL
1 tsp	garlic powder	5 mL
1 tsp	onion powder	5 mL

1. Place pork in a large pot. Add just enough water to cover. Bring to a boil over medium-high heat. Reduce heat and boil gently, stirring occasionally, until water and juices have evaporated, 15 to 20 minutes. Reduce heat to low. Add Red Enchilada Sauce, hot pepper flakes, oregano, cumin, garlic powder and onion powder. Mix well until all spices are well blended and sauce is heated through.

Carne Adovada Burritos

Makes 6 burritos

This flavorful red chile pork is delicious folded into a fresh flour tortilla and smothered in more red chile!

Tip

My family is always on the go so there are many times when I make burritos to go! We call them "hand-held" burritos. If you are making "hand-held" burritos, fold bottom edge of tortilla up over filling, then fold in both sides of the tortilla. Starting at folded bottom edge, roll up to enclose filling.

- Preheat oven to 375°F (190°C)
- Ovenproof plates

	Carne Adovada, warmed (see above)	
6	10-inch (25 cm) flour tortillas, skillet-warmed (page 75)	6
2 cups	Red Enchilada Sauce (page 63)	500 mL
1½ cups	shredded Cheddar cheese, divided	375 mL

1. To build burritos, divide meat mixture equally among tortillas, placing on bottom edge. Fold bottom edge of tortilla up over filling. Starting at folded bottom edge, roll up to enclose filling. Secure with a toothpick.

2. Place burritos seam side down on individual ovenproof plates. Spoon sauce over top, dividing equally, and sprinkle equally with cheese. Bake in preheated oven until cheese is melted and bubbly and burritos are heated through, 12 to 15 minutes.

Grilled Sirloin Burritos

Makes 4 burritos

This beefy burrito is a combination of grilled meat and sautéed vegetables.

Tip

Instead of grilling the steak, place it on a broiler pan and broil 2 to 3 inches (5 to 7.5 cm) away from the heat or sear in a large cast-iron skillet over medium-high heat for 3 to 4 minutes per side.

- Preheat greased barbecue grill to medium-high
- Preheat oven to 375°F (190°C)
- Ovenproof plates

1½ lbs	boneless beef top sirloin steak	750 g
2 tbsp	olive oil, divided	30 mL
	Kosher salt	
1	onion, sliced into ¼-inch (0.5 cm) thick rings	1
1	red bell pepper, julienned	1
1	orange bell pepper, julienned	1
	Salt and freshly ground black pepper	
4	10-inch (25 cm) flour tortillas, skillet-warmed (page 75)	4
2 cups	Green Enchilada Sauce (page 64) or Red Enchilada Sauce (page 63)	500 mL
1 cup	shredded Monterey Jack or Cheddar cheese	250 mL

1. Brush meat with 1 tbsp (15 mL) of the oil. Season with salt to taste. Grill steak, turning once, for 3 to 4 minutes per side, depending on the thickness of the steak, until medium-rare or until an internal temperature of 145°F (63°C) and well browned on surface. Transfer to a cutting board, tent with foil and let stand for 5 minutes. Thinly slice meat across the grain.

2. In a large skillet, heat remaining 1 tbsp (15 mL) of oil over medium heat. Add onion, red and orange bell peppers and salt and pepper to taste and cook, stirring, until peppers are tender-crisp and vegetables are slightly charred, 10 to 12 minutes. Remove from heat.

3. To build burritos, divide meat and onion mixture equally among tortillas. Fold bottom edge of tortilla up over filling. Starting at folded bottom edge, roll up to enclose filling. Secure with a toothpick.

4. Place burritos seam side down on individual ovenproof plates. Spoon sauce on top, dividing equally, and sprinkle with cheese. Bake in oven until cheese is melted and bubbly and burritos are heated through, 12 to 15 minutes.

Chorizo and Egg Burritos

Makes 4 burritos

Chorizo is a very savory Mexican sausage that is pungent and adds a lot of flavor to this little breakfast burrito. It is served in cafés throughout the Southwest.

- Preheat oven to 375°F (190°C)
- Ovenproof plates

1 tbsp	olive oil	15 mL
6 oz	fresh chorizo, removed from casing	175 g
8	eggs, slightly beaten	8
4	10-inch (25 cm) flour tortillas, skillet-warmed (page 75)	4
2 cups	shredded Monterey Jack or Cheddar cheese, divided	500 mL
2 cups	Green Enchilada Sauce (page 64) or Red Enchilada Sauce (page 63)	500 mL

1. In a large skillet, heat oil over medium heat. Add chorizo and fry, stirring and breaking up with a spoon if fresh, until well browned, 6 to 8 minutes. Add eggs and cook, stirring, until scrambled and set, 6 to 8 minutes. Remove from heat.

2. To build burritos, divide egg mixture equally among tortillas, placing on bottom edge. Top with 1 cup (250 mL) of the cheese, divided equally. Fold bottom edge of tortilla up over filling. Starting at folded bottom edge, roll up to enclose filling.

3. Place burritos seam side down on individual ovenproof plates. Spoon sauce on top, dividing equally, and sprinkle with remaining cheese. Bake in preheated oven until cheese is melted and bubbly and burritos are heated through, 12 to 15 minutes.

Potato, Egg and Chile Burritos

Makes 4 burritos

This is a generous breakfast burrito that will fill you up. The combination of egg and potato is a good balance of protein and carbs accented with chile for tons of flavor!

Tip

My family is always on the go so there are many times when I make burritos to go! We call them "hand-held" burritos. If you are making "hand-held" burritos, fold bottom edge of tortilla up over filling, then fold in both sides of the tortilla. Starting at folded bottom edge, roll up to enclose filling.

2 tbsp	olive oil, divided	30 mL
1	potato, cut into ¼-inch (0.5 cm) dice	1
	Salt	
½ cup	roasted green chile peppers (see page 98)	125 mL
6	eggs, lightly beaten	6
4	10-inch (25 cm) flour tortillas, skillet-warmed (page 75)	4
2 cups	shredded Cheddar cheese, divided	500 mL
2 cups	Green Enchilada Sauce (page 64) or Red Enchilada Sauce (page 63)	500 mL

1. In a medium skillet, heat 1 tbsp (15 mL) of oil over medium-high heat. Add potato and cook, covered, stirring occasionally, until potato is soft, 10 to 12 minutes. Remove lid and cook, stirring, until potato is soft, lightly browned and crispy, 8 to 10 minutes more. Season with salt to taste. Transfer to a bowl and set aside.

2. Reduce heat to medium-low. Add remaining 1 tbsp (15 mL) oil to skillet. Add chiles and cook, stirring, until chile is heated through, 2 to 3 minutes. Add eggs and cook, stirring, until set. Return potatoes to skillet and mix well.

3. To build burritos, divide egg mixture equally among tortillas, placing in center. Top with 1 cup (250 mL) of the cheese divided equally. Fold bottom edge of tortilla up over filling. Starting at folded bottom edge, roll up to enclose filling.

4. Place burritos seam side down on individual ovenproof plates. Spoon sauce on top, dividing equally, and sprinkle with remaining cheese. Bake in preheated oven until cheese is melted and bubbly and burritos are heated through, 12 to 15 minutes.

Refried Bean Tostadas

Makes 8 tostadas

A tostada is like an open-faced taco with beans, cheese and crispy greens layered on a crispy corn tortilla shell. It is a bit messy to eat, so make sure you have a fork nearby!

Tips

For tostada shells with reduced calories: Spray both sides of each tortilla lightly with nonstick cooking spray. Place on a baking sheet and bake in preheated 400°F (200°C) oven, turning once, until crispy and lightly browned, 4 to 6 minutes per side.

- Candy/deep-fry thermometer

	Vegetable oil	
8	6-inch (15 cm) corn tortillas	8
2 cups	Quick Refried Beans or Stove Top Refried Beans (page 100)	500 mL
1 cup	shredded Cheddar cheese	250 mL
2 cups	chopped romaine lettuce	500 mL
	Fiery Corn Salsa (page 59)	
½ cup	crumbled Cotija cheese (see Tips, page 108)	125 mL

1. In a deep fryer or deep heavy pot, heat 3 inches (7.5 cm) of oil to 350°F (180°C). Working with one tortilla at a time, gently fry each tortilla for about 2 minutes until crispy and hard. Using tongs, carefully turn tortilla over and fry for 1 minute more. Transfer to a paper towel-lined surface to drain. Adjust heat as necessary between tostada shells.

2. Place tostadas on individual serving plates. Divide beans equally among tostada shells, spreading to the edge of each shell. Top with equal amounts of Cheddar cheese and lettuce. Garnish with salsa and Cotija cheese.

Variation

Omit the Cotija cheese and substitute Tomato Table Salsa (page 57) for the Fiery Corn Salsa.

Grilled Beef Tostadas

Makes 8 tostadas

Crispy tostadas are yummy crowned with charred bits of beef. This is perfect for a relaxed gathering where everyone can make their own or select a favorite salsa.

Tip

I like to serve these tostadas with Green Chile and Jalapeño Salsa (page 58), Fiery Corn Salsa (page 59), Tomatillo Avocado Salsa (page 60) and Garlic and Jalapeño Relish (page 62).

- Preheat greased barbecue grill to medium-high
- Candy/deep-fry thermometer

	Vegetable oil	
8	6-inch (15 cm) corn tortillas	8
1 lb	beef skirt steak or minute steak	500 g
	Salt and freshly ground black pepper	
2 cups	Quick Refried Beans or Stove Top Refried Beans (page 100)	500 mL
2 cups	chopped green salad mix	500 mL
1 cup	crumbled Cotija or feta cheese	250 mL
1	tomato, seeded and diced	1

1. In a deep fryer or deep heavy pot, heat 3 inches (7.5 cm) of oil to 350°F (180°C). Working with one tortilla at a time, gently fry each tortilla for about 2 minutes until crispy and hard. Using tongs, carefully turn tortilla over and fry for 1 minute more. Transfer to a paper towel-lined surface to drain. Adjust heat as necessary between tostada shells.

2. Season both sides of beef skirt steak or minute steak with salt and pepper to taste. Grill meat, turning once, for 4 to 5 minutes per side for medium-rare. Transfer to a cutting board, tent with foil and let stand for 8 to 10 minutes. Cut meat across the grain into thin slices, then cut into bite-size pieces.

3. Place tostadas on individual serving plates. Divide beans equally among tostada shells, spreading to the edge of each shell. Top with equal amounts of salad mix, Cotija cheese and steak. Top with tomato and serve with a variety of salsas (see Tip, left).

Grilled Chicken Tostadas

Makes 8 tostadas		

Char-grilled chicken adds a texture and flavor that is savory and delicious. I like to be creative and add various fresh chopped vegetables as well.

Tip

Be creative and garnish with equal amounts of diced avocado, red onion, cilantro and/or diced jalapeño.

- Preheat greased barbecue grill to medium-high
- Candy/deep-fry thermometer

	Vegetable oil	
8	6-inch (15 cm) corn tortillas	8
1½ lbs	boneless skinless chicken breasts	750 g
2 tbsp	olive oil	30 mL
	Salt and freshly ground black pepper	
2 cups	Quick Refried Beans or Stove Top Refried Beans (page 100)	500 mL
1 cup	shredded Cheddar or Monterey Jack cheese	250 mL
2 cups	chopped green salad mix	500 mL

1. In a deep fryer or deep heavy pot, heat 3 inches (7.5 cm) of oil to 350°F (180°C). Working with one tortilla at a time, gently fry each tortilla for about 2 minutes until crispy and hard. Using tongs, carefully turn tortilla over and fry for 1 minute more. Transfer to a paper towel-lined surface to drain. Adjust heat as necessary between tostada shells.

2. Coat chicken breasts with olive oil. Season with salt and pepper. Grill chicken, turning once, until no longer pink inside, 6 to 8 minutes per side. Transfer to a cutting board and let stand for 6 to 8 minutes. Cut chicken into bite-size pieces.

3. Place tostadas on individual serving plates. Divide beans equally among tostada shells, spreading to the edge of each shell. Top with equal amounts of chicken, cheese and salad mix.

Variation

Shredded Chicken Tostadas: Instead of grilling chicken breasts, you can use 3 cups (750 mL) shredded leftover roasted chicken or Poached Chicken (page 153).

Stuffed Tostadas

Makes 8 tostadas

Crispy corn tortilla cups filled with beans and spicy meat are tasty and fun. They are overflowing with flavor and crowned with fresh lettuce, tomato and cheese. I like to bake my tortilla cups to reduce calories, but they can be fried instead.

- Preheat oven to 400°F (200°C)
- 4 deep ovenproof bowls

8	6-inch (15 cm) corn tortillas	8
	Vegetable oil cooking spray	
2 cups	Quick Refried Beans or Stove Top Refried Beans, warmed (page 100)	500 mL
	Carne Adovada (page 142)	
2 cups	shredded lettuce	500 mL
2	tomatoes, seeded and diced	2
2 cups	shredded Cheddar cheese	500 mL

1. Lightly coat tortillas with cooking spray on both sides. Place tortillas, 2 at a time, in a small, microwave-safe plastic bag and microwave on High for 15 seconds. Tortillas should be moist and pliable, but not too hot to handle. Remove from plastic bag. Fit each tortilla in deep bowl, carefully using your fingers to fold and mold the edges into a curvy shape. Place bowls in preheated oven immediately and bake until tortillas are crispy and golden brown, 10 to 12 minutes. Let cool in bowls. Transfer to individual serving plates.

2. Divide beans equally among tortilla cups. Top with Carne Adovada. Garnish equally with lettuce, tomatoes and cheese.

> ## Variations
> Substitute 2 cups (500 mL) shredded cooked beef (page 115) or shredded cooked chicken (page 153) for Carne Adovada.

Shredded Beef Tortas

Makes 4 sandwiches

These Mexican sandwiches are distinctively different from their American counterparts. Piled high with tender meat and garnished with a little Pico de Gallo and pickled jalapeño, they are spicy and yummy.

Tip

I like to use fresh baked round buns, about the size of your palm, from the bakery. You can use Bolillo rolls (page 76), hamburger buns or crusty buns.

2 cups	shredded cooked beef (page 115)	500 mL
	Salt and freshly ground black pepper	
4	soft round buns, split (see Tip, left)	4
¼ cup	mayonnaise	60 mL
1 cup	Pico de Gallo (page 56)	250 mL
1½ cups	shredded lettuce	375 mL
12	slices pickled jalapeño peppers	12
½ cup	shredded Monterey Jack cheese	125 mL
½ cup	shredded Cheddar Cheese	125 mL

1. In a skillet, heat beef over medium heat and season with salt and pepper to taste, stirring often, until meat is heated through. Remove from heat.

2. Lightly toast both sides of each bun. Spread cut side of bottom half of each bun with mayonnaise. Top with equal amounts of beef, Pico de Gallo and lettuce. Garnish with slices of jalapeños. Top with cheese and top with bun.

Beefy Avocado Tortas

Makes 4 sandwiches		

The sizzlin' charred sirloin makes this sandwich a favorite. Seasoned beef topped with loads of cheese and avocado nestled in a toasted bun is a crowd pleaser.

1 tbsp	olive oil	15 mL
1½ lbs	boneless beef sirloin steak, cut into bite-size pieces	750 g
1½ tsp	seasoned salt	7 mL
½ tsp	garlic powder	2 mL
4	soft round buns, split (see Tip, page 150)	4
¼ cup	mayonnaise	60 mL
½ cup	shredded Monterey Jack cheese	125 mL
½ cup	shredded Cheddar cheese	125 mL
1½ cups	shredded lettuce	375 mL
12	slices pickled jalapeño peppers	12
2	avocados, peeled and mashed	2

1. In a large skillet, heat oil over medium heat. Add meat, seasoned salt and garlic powder and cook, stirring, until all juices have evaporated and meat is slightly charred, 18 to 20 minutes. Remove from heat.

2. Lightly toast both sides of each bun. Spread cut side of bottom half of each bun with mayonnaise. Top with equal amounts of beef, cheese and lettuce. Garnish with slices of jalapeños. Spread cut side of each bun top with equal amounts of avocado and place on top of jalapeños.

Grilled Chicken Tortas

|||||||||||||||||||||||||||||||||||||||||||||||||||||||||||||||||||||||||||||||||||||||||||||

Makes 4 sandwiches

My family loves this tasty twist on grilled chicken. I spice it up with an easy infused mayonnaise for a mouthwatering sandwich.

|||||||||||||||||||||||||||||||||||||

● Preheat greased barbecue grill to medium-high

¼ cup	mayonnaise	60 mL
½ tsp	hot pepper flakes	2 mL
1½ lbs	skinless boneless chicken breasts	750 g
2 tbsp	olive oil	30 mL
	Salt and freshly ground black pepper	
4	soft round buns, split (see Tip, page 150)	4
2 cups	shredded lettuce	500 mL
1 cup	shredded Monterey Jack cheese	250 mL
2	avocados, peeled and mashed	2

1. In a small bowl, combine mayonnaise and hot pepper flakes. Set aside.

2. Coat chicken breasts with olive oil. Season with salt and pepper to taste. Grill chicken, turning once, until no longer pink inside, 6 to 8 minutes per side. Transfer to a cutting board and let stand for 6 to 8 minutes. Cut chicken into bite-size pieces.

3. Toast both sides of each bun. Spread cut side of bottom half of each bun with mayonnaise mixture. Top with equal amounts of chicken and lettuce. Top with cheese. Spread avocado on cut side of each bun top and place on top of cheese.

Shredded Chicken Tortas

This Mexican sandwich is spicy and delicious. The pickled jalapeños add heat while the cabbage slaw garnish balances the flavor and adds a fresh texture.

Tips

When I am pressed for time I pick up a roasted chicken from the deli section of my grocery store. Typically one 4-lb (2 kg) roasted chicken will yield approximately 4 cups (1 L) of diced chicken.

Chicken breasts are generally 5 oz (150 g) each. Once cooked and shredded, they yield about ½ cup (125 mL) of cooked chicken.

2 tbsp	olive oil	30 mL
3 tbsp	rice wine vinegar	45 mL
	Salt and freshly ground black pepper	
2 cups	shredded cabbage	500 mL
2 cups	shredded cooked chicken (see below)	500 mL
4	soft round buns, split (see Tip, page 150)	4
¼ cup	mayonnaise	60 mL
12	slices pickled jalapeño peppers	12
2	avocados, peeled and mashed	2

1. In a medium bowl, combine olive oil, vinegar, salt and pepper. Mix well. Add cabbage and toss until well coated. Cover and refrigerate until chilled, for at least 30 minutes or for up to 4 hours.

2. In a large skillet, heat chicken over medium heat and season with salt and pepper to taste, stirring often, until chicken is heated through, 8 to 10 minutes. Remove from heat.

3. Lightly toast both sides of each bun. Spread cut side of bottom half of each bun with mayonnaise. Top with equal amounts of chicken and cabbage mixture. Garnish with slices of jalapeños. Spread avocado on cut side of each bun top and place on top of jalapeños.

Poached Chicken

Place 1½ lbs (750 g) boneless skinless chicken breasts in a large pot and fill with enough water to cover the chicken by 2 inches (5 cm). Add 3 cloves garlic, chopped, and 1 onion, cut into quarters. Bring to a gentle boil over medium heat. Reduce heat and simmer until chicken is tender and no longer pink inside, 18 to 20 minutes. Transfer chicken to a bowl. Discard broth, garlic and onions. Use broth for another recipe. Let chicken cool for 10 to 12 minutes. Shred chicken with your fingers or two forks or dice according to the recipe. Use immediately or let cool completely and place in a resealable plastic bag. Refrigerate for up to 2 days or freeze for up to 4 months.

Red Chile Tamales

Makes 12 to 14 tamales

Tamales are a Mexican tradition that are typically served around the winter holidays. They are labor intensive but not too difficult. I like to make the meat filling ahead and then tamale making can be an activity for the day.

Tips

You can purchase a dried 16 oz (500 g) bag of corn husks in the ethnic section of your market or online.

Buy masa harina in the Mexican food section of your grocery store or online.

● Large pot with steam insert and lid

12 to 14	dried corn husks (see Tips, left)	12 to 14
3 cups	masa harina (see Tips, left)	750 mL
1 tsp	baking powder	5 mL
2½ cups	chicken broth	625 mL
¾ cup	lard	175 mL
	Salt	
	Carne Adovada (page 142)	

1. Submerge corn husks in water until soft and pliable, about 30 minutes. Remove from water and dry on paper towels (see Tips, right). Set up your assembly area with a cutting board, corn husks, bowl of masa and bowl of Carne Adovada filling.

2. In a medium bowl, combine masa harina and baking powder. Slowly add chicken broth and lard. Knead with hands until well blended, 3 to 5 minutes. It should have a pasty consistency. Set aside.

3. Place damp corn husk on cutting board or work surface with the narrow end closest to you and place another corn husk overlapping along the long edges with the wide end closest to you. Place ¼ cup (60 mL) masa mixture in the center of overlapped husks. Using a spoon, spread masa into a rectangle about ¼-inch (0.5 cm) thick over both corn husks.

4. Top masa with 1 tbsp (15 mL) of meat filling, spreading it down the center of the masa. Gently fold the right side of the corn husk toward the center then the left side. Fold one end of masa and meat filled tamale toward the center.

5. Repeat with remaining corn husks.

Tips

If masa is too sticky, use a corn husk to press masa into place.

You can add spices to your masa such as red chile powder or garlic powder.

6. In a large pot over medium-high heat, boil about 2 inches (5 cm) water. Place the steam insert in the pot. Place tamales in the pot with the folded end down, making sure that the tamales are not touching. Cover and steam until dough is firm around the meat filling, 45 minutes to 1 hour. To check for doneness the masa should pull away easily from the corn husks and should be firm and encase the filling.

Variation

For a meatless tamale that is rich and spicy, try Green Chile and Cheese Tamales. Follow Step 1 and 2. Substitute 2 cups (500 mL) shredded Monterey Jack cheese and 1 cup (250 mL) chopped roasted green chile, blended together, for the Carne Adovada. Continue with Step 3.

Ham and Jalapeño Tortas

Makes 4 sandwiches

Tortas can be customized to fit your taste buds. This is a unique combination that will remind you of a good old-fashioned ham sandwich.

4	soft round buns, split (see Tip, page 150)	4
½ cup	mayonnaise	125 mL
1 lb	deli-style ham, thinly sliced	500 g
1 cup	shredded Cheddar cheese	250 mL
12	slices pickled jalapeño peppers	12
2 cups	shredded lettuce	500 mL
2	avocados, peeled and mashed	2

1. Toast both sides of each bun. Spread cut sides of bottom half of each bun with mayonnaise. Top with equal amounts of ham and cheese. Top with jalapeño slices, then equal amounts of lettuce. Spread avocado on cut side of each bun top and place on top of lettuce.

Mexican Grill

Grilled Corn on the Cob

Makes 4 servings

Also known as *elote asado* or "roasted corn," this recipe is spicy, tangy and delicious. Blending butter with citrus and chile gives you a fiesta of flavor.

● Barbecue grill

4	ears corn in husks	4
½ cup	butter	125 mL
	Juice of 1 lime	
	Kosher salt	
1½ tbsp	hot pepper flakes	22 mL

1. In a large pot or bowl, soak corn in their husks in water to cover for 1 hour. Peel off all but a couple of layers of husk.

2. Preheat greased barbecue grill to medium-high heat.

3. Grill corn in their husks, turning occasionally, until corn is soft, for 15 to 20 minutes.

4. Meanwhile, in a small saucepan, melt butter over low heat. Remove from heat and stir in lime juice. Keep warm.

5. Let corn cool slightly and then use a hand towel to peel off the husks carefully. Place on a platter and brush generously with butter mixture equally over each ear of corn. Sprinkle with salt and pepper flakes.

Variation

For extra flavor, crumble 1 tbsp (15 mL) Cotija cheese on each ear of corn just before serving.

Spicy Grilled Vegetables

|||||||||||||||||||||||||||||||||||||||||||||||||||||||||||||||||||||||||||||||||||||||||||||||||||||||||||||

Makes 4 servings

Roasted vegetables add just the right amount of freshness to a plate of tacos, enchiladas or a Mexican grilled entrée. A little heat from the jalapeño kicks up the flavor.

- Preheat greased barbecue to medium-high heat
- Vegetable grilling grate or basket or heavy foil

¼ cup	olive oil	60 mL
1 tbsp	rice vinegar	15 mL
2	cloves garlic, minced	2
1 tbsp	minced Italian flat-leaf parsley	15 mL
2	red bell peppers, cut into quarters	2
1	green bell pepper, cut into quarters	1
3	jalapeño peppers, seeded and sliced lengthwise in half	3
1	onion, cut into ½-inch (1 cm) thick slices	1
1	zucchini, cut crosswise into 1-inch (2.5 cm) thick slices	1
1	small yellow summer squash (zucchini) or small eggplant, cut crosswise into 1-inch (2.5 cm) thick slices	1
	Kosher salt	

1. Place vegetable grate or basket or a large piece foil on the grill to heat.

2. In a small bowl, combine oil, vinegar, garlic and parsley.

3. Brush vegetables with oil mixture. Place in preheated vegetable grate or on foil and grill, turning once, until vegetables are tender-crisp, 4 to 6 minutes per side. Season with kosher salt and grill, turning once, until tender, 6 to 8 minutes more. Serve immediately.

Variation

For additional flavor, add 1 tbsp (15 mL) minced cilantro to oil mixture. For a spicier flavor, add 1 tsp (5 mL) chipotle chile powder to oil mixture.

Grilled Chile Peppers

Makes 4 to
6 servings

I love the way spicy chile, creamy cheese and the smoke of the grill go together. The savory taste of bacon wraps this chile up in style.

- Preheat greased barbecue to medium heat
- 12 toothpicks, soaked in water for 20 minutes

6	Anahiem or New Mexico whole green chiles, roasted and peeled (page 98)	6
1 lb	Monterey Jack cheese or Asadero cheese	500 g
6	slices bacon	6

1. Slice each roasted chile in half lengthwise. Using a spoon, scoop out seeds and ribs from chiles, leaving stems intact.

2. Cut cheese into six 4- by-1 inch (10 by 2.5 cm) pieces. Gently stuff each chile with 1 piece of cheese. Wrap each chile, from the stem to the end, with a slice of bacon and secure with toothpicks at both ends.

3. Grill, turning once, until cheese is melted and bacon is crispy, about 6 minutes per side. Transfer to a platter. Slice in half or into thirds crosswise when serving as an appetizer or serve whole for a side dish.

Chipotle Chicken Skewers

Makes 4 servings

These glazed chicken skewers combine a thick, smoky sauce with a hint of honey for a distinctive and delicious result.

Tip

You can find cans of chipotle chile peppers in adobo sauce in the Mexican food section at many grocery stores or at Latin food stores.

- Preheat greased barbecue grill to medium-high heat
- Four 10- to 12-inch (25 to 30 cm) flat metal skewers

¼ cup	liquid honey	60 mL
2 tbsp	puréed chipotle chile peppers in adobo sauce (see Tip, left)	30 mL
2 tbsp	olive oil	30 mL
1½ lbs	boneless skinless chicken breasts, cut into bite-size pieces	750 g
	Salt and freshly ground black pepper	

1. In a medium bowl, whisk together honey, chiles and oil. Set aside.

2. Divide chicken equally and thread on skewers. Lightly season chicken with salt and pepper.

3. Grill chicken skewers, turning once, until no longer pink inside, 6 to 8 minutes per side. Brush chicken generously with glaze and grill for 1 minute on each side. Let stand for 6 to 8 minutes. Serve immediately.

Spicy Steak Tampico (page 165) with Stove Top Refried Beans (page 100), Green Chile and Herb Rice (page 98) and Festive Mexican Slaw (page 107)

Grilled Shrimp with Avocado Butter (page 161)

Enchilada Casserole (page 174)

Beef Fajitas (page 175)

Huevos Rancheros (page 178)

Pomegranate Margarita (page 188)
and Mexican Mojito (page 194)

Bizcochitos (page 203) and Margarita Pie (page 209)

Mexican Chocolate Cakes (page 211)

Grilled Shrimp with Avocado Butter

Makes 4 servings

- Barbecue grill
- Food processor
- Four 10- to 12-inch (25 to 30 cm) flat metal skewers

Lightly marinated shrimp are simple but amazingly flavorful. Rich avocado butter adds a balance in texture and taste.

Tip

I like using a blend of spices to shorten my ingredient list. Creole seasoning has a combination of onion, garlic, cayenne pepper, oregano, salt and pepper. There are many good blends on the market, so you can find a favorite.

Avocado Butter

3	avocados, cut in quarters or into chunks	3
2	clove garlic, minced	2
2 tbsp	freshly squeezed lime juice	30 mL
2 tbsp	olive oil	30 mL
	Kosher or sea salt	
	Juice of 2 limes (about 1/4 cup/60 mL)	
1	clove garlic, minced	1
1 tbsp	Creole seasoning (see Tip, left)	15 mL
1/2 tsp	cayenne pepper	2 mL
2 tbsp	olive oil	30 mL
16	jumbo shrimp, peeled and deveined (see Tip, page 134)	16

1. *Avocado Butter:* In a food processor, combine avocados, garlic, lime juice and olive oil and process until smooth. Add salt to taste. Serve immediately or transfer to an airtight container and refrigerate, stirring occasionally, for 30 minutes or for up to 2 hours.

2. In a medium bowl, whisk lime juice, garlic, Creole seasoning, cayenne and oil until well blended. Add shrimp and toss gently. Cover and refrigerate for at least 30 minutes or for up to 2 hours.

3. Meanwhile, preheat barbecue grill to medium-high.

4. Remove shrimp from marinade and discard marinade. Thread 4 shrimp on each skewer.

5. Grill shrimp, turning once, until shrimp are pink and opaque, 3 to 4 minutes per side. Transfer to a platter. Gently remove from skewers and serve with Avocado Butter.

Grilled Tilapia Veracruz

Makes 4 servings		

This entrée is infused with Spanish and Mediterranean flavors. A lightly grilled fillet topped with olives, capers and tomato is full of color. The taste of jalapeño is a flavorful accent.

● Preheat barbecue grill to medium-high heat

3 tbsp	olive oil, divided	45 mL
1	onion, thinly sliced	1
2	cloves garlic, minced	2
¼ cup	dry white wine	60 mL
¼ cup	chopped green olives	60 mL
1	tomato, seeded and diced	1
¼ cup	drained sliced pickled jalapeño peppers	60 mL
1 tbsp	minced drained capers	15 mL
Pinch	granulated sugar	Pinch
4	skinless tilapia, snapper or cod fillets (each 6 oz/175 g)	4
1 tsp	kosher salt	5 mL
½ tsp	freshly ground black pepper	2 mL
2 tbsp	freshly squeezed lemon juice	30 mL

1. In a skillet, heat 2 tbsp (30 mL) of the oil over medium-high heat. Sauté onion and garlic until onion is transparent, 6 to 8 minutes. Reduce heat to medium and add wine, olives, tomato, jalapeños, capers and sugar. Reduce heat and simmer, stirring often, until vegetables are heated through, 12 to 15 minutes. Drain off excess liquid and keep warm.

2. Rinse tilapia and pat dry with paper towel. Brush fillets with remaining 1 tbsp (15 mL) of oil on both sides. Sprinkle with salt and pepper. Grill, turning once, until fish flakes easily with a fork, 4 minutes per side. Transfer to a platter, baste with lemon juice and garnish with olive mixture.

Grilled Tilapia Fillets

Makes 4 servings

Lightly grilling this fish with lemon and spices adds to the delicate richness and flavor of tilapia. A citrusy salsa laced with creamy avocado crowns this entrée perfectly.

● Barbecue grill

2 tbsp	olive oil	30 mL
2 tbsp	freshly squeezed lemon juice	30 mL
1 tbsp	minced cilantro	15 mL
1 tsp	seasoned salt	5 mL
4	skinless tilapia fillets (each 6 oz/175 g)	4
	Tomatillo Avocado Salsa (page 60)	

1. In a medium bowl, whisk together oil, lemon juice, cilantro and salt until well blended.

2. Place fillets in a shallow glass baking dish and pour marinade over fillets. Cover and refrigerate for at least 30 minutes or for up to 2 hours.

3. Preheat greased barbecue grill to medium-high heat.

4. Wrap fillets in foil and grill fillets, turning once, until fish flakes easily with a fork, about 4 minutes per side. Serve on individual plates. Garnish with Tomatillo Avocado Salsa.

Carne Asada

Makes 4 to
6 servings

Carne asada, or grilled meat, is the king of Mexican grilling. A marinade of citrus and chile flavors blends perfectly with the big beefy flavor of this steak.

Tip

I serve Carne Asada topped with avocado slices. Serve it with Stove Top Refried Beans (page 100), Spanish Rice (page 97) and fresh flour tortillas (pages 72 and 73) for an authentic Mexican meal.

● Barbecue grill

Marinade

	Juice of 3 lemons	
3	cloves garlic, minced	3
½ cup	drained sliced pickled jalapeño peppers	125 mL
1 tbsp	minced red bell pepper	15 mL
½ cup	teriyaki sauce	125 mL
1 tbsp	granulated sugar	15 mL
2 tsp	kosher salt	10 mL
2 lbs	beef skirt steak or minute steaks (see Tip, page 125)	1 kg
¼ cup	cilantro, torn into pieces	60 mL
2	limes, each cut into 6 wedges	2

1. *Marinade:* In a large resealable plastic bag, combine lemon juice, garlic, jalapeños, bell pepper, teriyaki sauce, sugar and salt until sugar and salt have dissolved.

2. Add meat and cilantro. Seal bag and work marinade through meat with your fingers. Refrigerate for at least 2 hours or for up to 6 hours.

3. Preheat greased barbecue grill to medium. Remove meat from marinade, discarding marinade. Grill meat, turning once, for 4 to 5 minutes per side for medium-rare. Transfer to a cutting board, tent with foil and let stand for 8 to 10 minutes. Carve meat across the grain into thin slices. Serve with lime wedges to squeeze over top.

Variation

For Pollo Asada (grilled chicken), substitute 2 lbs (1 kg) boneless skinless chicken breasts for beef and grill until no longer pink inside, 6 to 8 minutes per side.

Spicy Steak Tampico

Makes 4 servings

This is simplicity in grilling! I love grilling a choice steak then lavishing it with fresh roasted green chile and rich melted cheese. Steak Tampico is the perfect entrée served with beans and rice.

- Preheat greased barbecue grill to medium-high
- Instant-read thermometer
- Ovenproof plates

4	beef tenderloin medallions (each 6 oz/175 g and ¾ inch/2 cm thick)	4
2 tbsp	olive oil	30 mL
	Seasoned salt and freshly ground black pepper	
1 cup	roasted green chile peppers (see page 98)	250 mL
1 cup	shredded Monterey Jack cheese	250 mL

1. Brush steaks thoroughly with olive oil. Season with salt and pepper.

2. Place medallions on preheated grill, close lid and grill, turning once, until an instant-read thermometer registers 145°F (63°C) for medium rare, 5 to 8 minutes per side. Transfer to a plate, tent with foil and let stand for 10 minutes.

3. Preheat broiler with rack 3 to 4 inches (7.5 to 10 cm) away from heat. Place steaks on individual ovenproof plates. Top each steak with equal amounts of chile and cheese. Broil until cheese melts, about 2 minutes. Serve immediately.

Variation

In place of the beef tenderloin, substitute four 6-oz (175 g) portions beef top sirloin steak, each 1-inch (2.5 cm) thick. For the most tender and juicy results choose a high-quality, well-aged sirloin.

Margarita Chicken

Makes 4 servings

This chicken recipe, with its citrusy flavors and a little dash of tequila, gives you all the flavors of the Mexican grill. I like this entrée served fresh off the grill as a main dish or sliced and wrapped up in a fresh corn tortilla and crowned with a fresh salsa.

Tip

There are a variety of orange liqueurs on the market such as Triple Sec, Cointreau or Grand Marnier. Experiment and find a favorite. I prefer the French liqueur, Cointreau.

● Barbecue grill

Marinade

	Juice of 3 limes	
2 tbsp	olive oil	30 mL
3	cloves garlic, minced	3
3 tbsp	tequila	45 mL
3 tbsp	orange-flavored liqueur (see Tip, left)	45 mL
2 tbsp	liquid honey	30 mL
1 tbsp	minced cilantro	15 mL
4	boneless skinless chicken breasts	4

1. *Marinade:* In a large resealable plastic bag, combine lime juice, olive oil, garlic, tequila, liqueur, honey and cilantro.

2. Add chicken. Seal bag and work marinade through chicken with your fingers. Refrigerate chicken for at least 2 hours or for up to 6 hours.

3. Preheat greased barbecue grill to medium-high heat. Remove chicken from marinade, discarding marinade. Grill chicken, turning once, until no longer pink inside, 6 to 8 minutes per side. Let stand for 6 to 8 minutes. Serve immediately whole or slice crosswise.

Enchiladas, Fajitas and Other Favorites

Red Chile Enchiladas

Makes 4 to
6 servings

Fresh corn tortillas stuffed with a beefy filling and smothered in a chile sauce melts in your mouth. I fix enchiladas a lot during the winter months. They can be served as a side dish or an entrée. Customize your enchiladas with a variety of fillings and garnishes.

Tip

For a lighter version, omit oil and heat corn tortillas in the microwave. Place 4 tortillas in a small resealable plastic bag and seal. Microwave on High for 25 to 45 seconds (depending on the power of your microwave). Remove from plastic bag. The tortillas should be warm and pliable. If you leave them in too long they will be too hot to handle and will be overdone.

- 13- by 9-inch (33 by 23 cm) glass baking dish, greased

	Oil	
12	6-inch (15 cm) corn tortillas	12
1½ lbs	ground beef	750 g
2 cups	Red Enchilada Sauce or store-bought (page 63)	500 mL
1 cup	shredded Cheddar cheese	250 mL
1 cup	shredded Monterey Jack cheese	250 mL
½ cup	sliced black olives	125 mL
4	green onions, green parts only, chopped	4

1. In a medium skillet, heat 1-inch (2.5 cm) oil over medium-high heat. Using tongs, carefully dip each tortilla into oil until tortilla bubbles and is heated through, about 1 minute. Transfer to paper towels to drain. Repeat with remaining tortillas.

2. In another large skillet over medium heat, cook beef, stirring and breaking up with a spoon, until browned and no longer pink, about 12 minutes. Set aside.

3. Place ¼ cup (60 mL) ground beef at end of each tortilla. Roll up and place seam side down in prepared baking dish. Top rolled enchiladas with sauce and Cheddar and Monterey Jack cheeses.

Tip

Enchiladas can be garnished with a variety of toppings. I often put out small bowls of sliced olives; green onions, green parts only; sour cream; diced tomato; chopped cilantro, and shredded lettuce. In certain areas of the Southwest, garnishing red and green enchiladas with toasted pecan pieces is popular, adding texture and flavor.

4. Bake in preheated oven until enchiladas are heated through and cheese is melted and bubbly, 20 to 25 minutes. Let stand for 8 to 10 minutes. Garnish with olives and green onions (see Tip, left).

Variations

Red Enchiladas with Shredded Beef: Substitute 3 cups (750 mL) cooked shredded beef (page 115) for the ground beef.

Vegetarian Red Enchiladas: Substitute 3 cups (750 mL) Creamy Corn, Chile and Squash (page 96) for the ground beef.

Green Chile Chicken Enchiladas

| Makes 4 to 6 servings |

Enchiladas come from the heart of Mexican cooking. The green chile sauce adds a smooth complex flavor yet they are so simple to make. They are a great "make ahead" entrée.

Tip

For a lighter version, omit oil and heat corn tortillas in the microwave. Place 4 tortillas in a small resealable plastic bag and seal. Microwave on High for 25 to 45 seconds (depending on the power of your microwave). Remove from plastic bag. The tortillas should be warm and pliable. If you leave them in too long they will be too hot to handle and will be overdone.

- Preheat oven to 350°F (180°C)
- 13- by 9-inch (33 by 23 cm) glass baking dish, greased

1 tbsp	olive oil	15 mL
2	cloves garlic, minced	2
½ cup	roasted green chile peppers (see page 98)	125 mL
1	onion, diced	1
¼ cup	chicken broth	60 mL
3 cups	diced roasted chicken (see page 153)	750 mL
	Oil	
12	6-inch (15 cm) corn tortillas, skillet-warmed (page 74)	12
2 cups	Green Enchilada Sauce or store-bought (page 64)	500 mL
1 cup	shredded Cheddar cheese	250 mL
1 cup	shredded Monterey Jack cheese	250 mL

1. In a large skillet, heat oil over medium heat. Add garlic and cook, stirring, until tender, about 1 minute. Add chiles, onion and broth and cook, stirring, until onion is translucent, 4 to 6 minutes. Add chicken and simmer, stirring occasionally, until chicken is heated through, 2 to 3 minutes.

2. In a medium skillet, heat 1-inch (2.5 cm) oil over medium-high heat. Using tongs, carefully dip each tortilla into the oil until tortilla bubbles and is heated through, about 1 minute. Transfer to paper towels to drain. Repeat with remaining tortillas.

3. Place ¼ cup (60 mL) chicken mixture at end of each tortilla. Roll up and place seam side down in baking dish. Top rolled enchiladas with sauce and Cheddar and Monterey Jack cheeses.

4. Bake in preheated oven until enchiladas are heated through and cheese is melted and bubbly, 20 to 25 minutes.

Variations

Green Chile Shrimp Enchiladas: Substitute 3 cups (750 mL) of cooked chopped shrimp for the chicken and heat for 2 to 3 minutes.

Green Chile Vegetarian Enchiladas: Omit oil, garlic, chile broth and chicken. Substitute 3 cups (750 mL) Creamy Corn Chile and Squash (page 96) and heat in Step 1. Continue with Step 2.

Simply Stacked Enchiladas

||||||||||||||||||||||||||||||||||||||||||||||||||||||||||||||||||||||||||||||||||||||||||||||||||||||||||||||||||||||||||||||||

<table>
<tr><td>Makes 4 servings</td></tr>
</table>

This is a quick meal for busy weeknights. I literally stand by the stove and serve everyone up one at a time. Place each plate in the oven to melt and it's done.

||||||||||||||||||||||||||||||||||||||||||||||||||||

Tip

You can also microwave each plate on Medium-High (70%) power in one-minute intervals until heated through.

- Preheat oven to 375°F (190°C)
- 4 ovenproof plates

2 cups	Red Enchilada Sauce or store-bought (page 63)	500 mL
12	6-inch (15 cm) corn tortillas, micro-warmed (page 74)	12
½ cup	diced onion	125 mL
2 cups	shredded Cheddar or Asadero Cheese	500 mL
2 cups	shredded iceberg lettuce	500 mL
1 cup	chopped seeded tomato	250 mL

1. In a medium saucepan over low heat, warm enchilada sauce. Using tongs, dip tortillas, one at a time, in sauce, allowing excess sauce to drip off into the pan. Place 4 tortillas on individual plates. Top each tortilla with about 1 tbsp (15 mL) of onion and cheese. Layer with remaining tortillas, onion and cheese so there are three layers. Top with remaining cheese.

2. Bake in preheated oven until cheese is completely melted and heated through, 8 to 10 minutes.

3. Garnish each plate with equal amounts of lettuce and tomato.

Variations

Beef Stacked Enchiladas: For a heartier dish, add 12 oz (375 g) ground beef, cooked and crumbled, to each plate after the second layer. Finish stacking with the last tortilla as directed.

Green Stacked Enchiladas: Substitute 2 cups (500 mL) Green Enchilada Sauce or store-bought (page 64) for Red Enchilada Sauce.

Green Chicken Stacked Enchiladas: Add ½ cup (125 mL) cooked and chopped or shredded chicken (page 153) to each plate after the second layer. Finish stacking with the last tortilla as directed.

New Mexico Stacked Enchiladas: New Mexicans like this style for breakfast, lunch and dinner. After baking, top each stack with an egg, cooked to order. Omit the lettuce and tomato.

Sour Cream Chicken Enchiladas

Makes 4 to 6 servings

This is a Mexican American favorite that I grew up on. Some might even call it Tex-Mex cooking. The creamy chicken filling creates a mouthwatering enchilada.

Tip

I like to assemble these enchiladas a day ahead. Follow Steps 1 through 4. Cover and refrigerate overnight. When ready to serve, let stand at room temperature for up to 15 minutes then continue with Step 5.

● Preheat 350°F (180°C)
● 13- by 9-inch (33 by 23 cm) glass baking dish, greased

2 tbsp	chicken broth	30 mL
2	cloves garlic, minced	2
1½ cups	roasted green chile peppers (see page 98)	375 mL
2 cups	shredded cooked chicken (page 153)	500 mL
2 cups	sour cream	500 mL
1	can (10¾ oz/284 mL) condensed cream of chicken soup	1
	Salt and freshly ground black pepper	
10	8- to 10-inch (20 to 25 cm) flour tortillas, skillet-warmed (page 75)	10
1¾ cups	shredded Cheddar cheese, divided	425 mL
	Cooking spray	
4	green onions, green parts only, minced	4

1. In a large skillet over medium heat, combine chicken broth, garlic and green chiles and cook, stirring, for 1 minute. Add chicken and cook until heated through, 2 to 3 minutes. Set aside.

2. In a large bowl, whisk together sour cream and condensed soup. Add chicken mixture and mix well. Add salt and pepper to taste. Set aside 1 cup (250 mL) of chicken mixture.

3. To build enchiladas, divide remaining chicken mixture among tortillas, placing at end of each tortilla. Sprinkle each with 1 tbsp (15 mL) of the cheese. Roll up and place seam side down in baking dish.

4. Lightly spray the ends of each rolled tortilla with cooking spray. Spread the remaining chicken mixture equally down the center so the ends are exposed and turn golden when baked. Top with remaining cheese.

5. Bake in preheated oven until tortillas are golden brown on the edges, cheese is melted and enchiladas are heated through, 25 to 30 minutes. Garnish with onions and serve immediately.

Enchilada Casserole

This is a wonderful make-ahead dish, great for potlucks. I love the green enchilada sauce with layers of chicken in between. However, for a completely different flavor try the red enchilada sauce with a beefy filling.

Tips

The Red or Green Enchilada Sauce recipe makes 2 cups (500 mL). For this recipe, add 1 cup (250 mL) water to get the 3 cups (750 mL) needed. This will make the sauce a bit thinner but it works well in this recipe.

Enchiladas can be garnished with a variety of toppings. I often put out small bowls of sliced olives; green onions, green parts only; sour cream; diced tomato; chopped cilantro; and shredded lettuce. In certain areas of the Southwest garnishing red and green enchiladas with toasted pecan pieces is popular, adding texture and flavor.

- Preheat oven to 350°F (180°C)
- 13- by 9-inch (33 by 23 cm) glass baking dish

24	6-inch (15 cm) corn tortillas, micro-warmed (page 74)	24
3 cups	Red or Green Enchilada Sauce or store-bought (pages 63 and 64), divided (see Tips, left)	750 mL
2 cups	diced cooked chicken	500 mL
3 cups	shredded Monterey Jack or Cheddar cheese	750 mL
1	onion, diced	1
1 cup	shredded lettuce	250 mL
½ cup	sliced black olives	125 mL
1	tomato, seeded and diced	1

1. Place 6 tortillas in the bottom of baking dish, overlapping as necessary. Top with 1 cup (250 mL) of the sauce, spreading to the outer edges of tortillas. Top with half of the chicken and 1 cup (250 mL) of the cheese, spreading to the outer edges of the tortillas. Garnish with one-third of the onion. Layer 6 more tortillas, sauce, the remaining chicken and half each of the remaining cheese and onion. Top with remaining 6 tortillas and remaining sauce, cheese and onion.

2. Bake in preheated oven until golden brown, 30 to 40 minutes. Let stand for 5 to 8 minutes. Cut into 6 equal squares and serve on individual plates. Garnish with lettuce, olives and tomatoes.

Variation

In Step 1, replace the diced cooked chicken with 2 cups (500 mL) ground beef, cooked and crumbled.

Beef Fajitas

||||||||||||||||||||||||||||||||||||||||||||||||||||||||||||||||||||||||||||||

Makes 4 servings			

Fajitas have become part of the North American Mexican food culture. They are quick to make and fun to eat. I like my fajitas tender and medium-rare. Skirt steak teamed with fresh vegetables is delicious yet simple to make.

1½ lbs	beef skirt steak	750 g
3 tbsp	olive oil, divided	45 mL
	Kosher salt	
	Juice of 1 lime	
1	onion, sliced into thick rings	1
1	each red and orange bell peppers, julienned	1
	Salt and freshly ground black pepper	
½ cup	sour cream	125 mL
	Pico de Gallo (page 56)	
	Classic Guacamole (page 51)	
	Flour tortillas	

1. Brush meat with 1 tbsp (15 mL) of the oil. Season with salt to taste. In a large skillet over medium-high heat, add 1 tbsp (15 mL) of oil and heat for 1 minute. Add steak and cook until medium-rare and well browned on surface, 3 to 4 minutes per side, depending on the thickness of the steak. Let stand for 5 minutes. Thinly slice meat across the grain.

2. In a large skillet, heat remaining 1 tbsp (15 mL) of oil over medium heat. Add onion, red and orange bell peppers and salt and pepper to taste and cook, stirring, until peppers are tender-crisp, 8 to 10 minutes. Add meat and cook until vegetables are slightly charred and steak is heated through, 2 to 3 minutes. Splash steak with lime juice. Serve immediately with sour cream, Pico de Gallo and Guacamole and fresh flour tortillas.

Variations

Chicken Fajitas: Substitute 1½ lbs (750 g) boneless skinless chicken breasts, sliced into strips (see Tip, page 123) for the beef in Step 1. Cook, stirring, until chicken is no longer pink inside and juices have evaporated, 12 to 14 minutes. Transfer to a bowl and set aside. Continue with Step 2.

Shrimp Fajitas: Omit chicken and substitute 24 medium shrimp, peeled and deveined. Continue with Step 2, cooking, stirring constantly, until shrimp are pink and opaque, 4 to 6 minutes.

Chicken Mole

|||||||||||||||||||||||||||||||||||||||||||||||||||||||||||||||||||||||||||||||||||||||||||||||||

Chicken served with a
richly flavored sauce is
popular in many parts
of Mexico. The earthy,
sweet flavor of the
sauce defines this dish.

|||||||||||||||||||||||||||||||||||||||||||||

Tip

Add a pinch of cinnamon
and ½ tsp (2 mL) granulated
sugar to the sauce with the
spices for a sweeter version.
Sprinkle finished dish with
toasted sesame seeds.

- Preheat oven to 350°F (180°C)
- 13- by 9-inch (33 by 23 cm) casserole dish, greased

2 cups	Red Enchilada Sauce (page 63)	500 mL
1 tsp	hot pepper flakes	5 mL
1 tsp	dried oregano	5 mL
1 tsp	ground cumin	5 mL
1 tsp	garlic powder	5 mL
1 tsp	onion powder	5 mL
1½ oz	semisweet chocolate, chopped into small pieces	45 g
3 tbsp	olive oil	45 mL
4- to 5-lb	whole chicken, cut into 8 pieces	2 to 2.5 kg
	Salt and freshly ground black pepper	

1. In a saucepan, heat sauce over medium heat until
   bubbly. Stir in hot pepper flakes, oregano, cumin,
   garlic powder and onion powder. Reduce heat and
   simmer, stirring often, until flavors are blended, 3 to
   5 minutes. Reduce heat to low and stir in chocolate
   until melted. Set aside.

2. In a large pot, heat oil over medium-high heat.
   Add chicken pieces, in batches to avoid crowding,
   and brown, turning once, for 3 to 4 minutes per
   side. Lightly season with salt and pepper. Transfer
   to prepared casserole dish. Repeat with remaining
   chicken, adjusting heat as necessary between batches.

3. Spread sauce evenly over chicken. Bake in preheated
   oven until juices run clear when chicken is pierced,
   about 45 minutes. Serve immediately.

Burrito Bowls

Makes 4 serving

I love these little bowls of goodness. This fun entrée is layers of flavor. It starts with rice on the bottom, then a meat or chicken filling, beans and your favorite garnishes. I like to serve this buffet-style and let everyone make their burrito bowl just the way they like it. It is a fun dish to serve at a tailgate party.

Tip

I like to offer a variety of additional garnishes, such as diced tomato and chopped cilantro, for diners to add to their bowls.

2 cups	Spanish Rice (page 97) or Green Chile and Herb Rice (page 98) warmed	500 mL
2 cups	Carne Adovada (shredded cooked beef) (page 142) or shredded cooked chicken (page 153) warmed	500 mL
1 cup	cooked Basic Pinto or Black Beans (page 99), drained and warmed	250 mL
1 cup	Salsa Verde (page 58), Pico de Gallo, (page 56), Roasted Tomato Salsa (page 56) or Fiery Corn Salsa (page 59)	250 mL
1 cup	shredded Asadero or Monterey Jack cheese	250 mL
¼ cup	Classic Guacamole (page 51) or store-bought	60 mL

1. Divide rice equally into each of 4 serving bowls. Top with equal amounts of beef, beans and salsa.

2. Garnish with equal amounts of cheese and guacamole and serve immediately.

Huevos Rancheros

Makes 4 servings	

This traditional ranch-style breakfast dish is a combination of eggs served on fried corn tortillas smothered in a cooked salsa or sauce. I serve them with a side of refried beans.

- Preheat oven to 150°F (70°C)
- Ovenproof serving plates

3 tbsp	oil, divided	45 mL
8	6-inch (15 cm) corn tortillas	8
2 cups	Roasted Tomato Salsa (page 56)	500 mL
4	eggs	4
½ cup	shredded Cheddar cheese	125 mL

1. Place serving plates in preheated oven to warm.

2. In a large skillet over high heat, add 2 tbsp (30 mL) of the oil and heat for 1 minute. Using tongs, carefully dip each tortilla into the oil until tortilla bubbles and is heated through, about 1 minute. Transfer to paper towels to drain. Place 2 tortillas slightly overlapping each other on each warmed plate. Return to oven.

3. In a medium saucepan over medium heat, heat salsa until bubbly, 5 to 7 minutes.

4. In another skillet, add remaining 1 tbsp (15 mL) of oil and scramble or fry eggs separately, as desired. Place each egg on top of tortillas on each plate and smother with salsa. Sprinkle with cheese. Return to oven and bake until cheese is slightly melted, 3 to 4 minutes.

Variation

I love this version with a rich enchilada sauce, red or green. Substitute Red Enchilada Sauce (page 63) or Green Enchilada Sauce (page 64) for the Roasted Tomato Salsa.

Chile Tortillas

Makes 4 servings

Basically this traditional dish (*Chilaquiles*) is fried corn tortilla chips cooked in red or green salsa or enchilada sauce. It can be garnished with eggs, meat and cheeses and served anytime of the day.

2 tbsp	olive oil	30 mL
2 cups	Salsa Verde (page 58) or Tomato Table Salsa (page 57)	500 mL
36	Fresh Tortilla Chips (corn) (page 34) or store-bought tortilla chips	36
1 cup	crumbled Cotija cheese	250 mL
1	onion, chopped	1
¼ cup	minced cilantro	60 mL
1	avocado, diced	1

1. In a large skillet, heat oil over medium-high heat. Add salsa and heat until bubbly, 5 to 7 minutes. Using tongs, gradually add chips, turning until well coated on both sides and cooking until some chips become soft, 3 to 4 minutes. Some will remain crispy.

2. Divide mixture equally among serving plates. Garnish with equal amounts of cheese, onion, cilantro and avocado.

Variations

Substitute Red Enchilada Sauce (page 63) for the salsa.

Breakfast Chilaquillas: Follow Steps 1 and 2. Top each serving with an egg, cooked to order.

Stuffed Sopapillas

Makes 4 servings

Enjoy a savory filling in these fried pastries. Sopapillas puff up into a golden pocket that you can fill with meats, cheeses and fresh garnishes.

½	recipe Sopapillas (page 81)	½
1 lb	ground beef	500 g
½ tsp	ground cumin	2 mL
	Salt and freshly ground pepper	
2 cups	shredded lettuce	500 mL
1 cup	shredded Monterey Jack cheese	250 mL
1	tomato, seeded and diced	1
1	onion, chopped	1

1. In a large skillet over medium heat, cook beef, stirring and breaking up with a spoon, until browned and no longer pink, about 12 minutes. Drain off excess fat. Add cumin and salt and pepper to taste. Remove from heat.

2. To build stuffed sopapillas, slice open each sopapilla at one end. Divide meat equally and place inside sopapillas. Stuff with equal amounts of lettuce, cheese, tomato and onion.

Beverages and Cocktails

Cinnamon Rice Milk

Known as *horchata* in Mexico, this is a smooth milky (yet dairy-free) delight that is spiced with cinnamon and a hint of almond. The ground rice gives it a slightly thicker texture. It can be served agua fresca–style, which means over ice, or steaming hot.

Tips

To serve warm: Omit ice. Transfer to a medium saucepan over medium heat. Cover until heated through, 6 to 8 minutes.

Horchata keeps covered and refrigerated for up to 3 days.

- Blender
- Cotton cheesecloth

½ cup	white rice, uncooked	125 mL
5½ cups	warm water, divided	1.375 L
1 cup	blanched almonds	250 mL
½ tsp	ground cinnamon	2 mL
½ tsp	lime zest	2 mL
1 cup	granulated sugar	250 mL
1 tsp	Mexican vanilla	5 mL
	Ice	
4	pieces (about 2 inches/5 cm) cinnamon sticks	4

1. Place rice in a blender and blend until powdery.

2. In a medium bowl, combine rice with 1½ cups (375 mL) of the warm water, almonds, cinnamon and lime zest. Cover and let stand at room temperature overnight. Transfer rice mixture to a blender and add 2 cups (500 mL) of warm water. Cover and blend until mixture is smooth.

3. Line a mesh strainer with two layers of 100% cotton cheesecloth. Poor rice mixture through cheesecloth. When liquid has passed through, gather up the cheesecloth and squeeze remaining liquid into the bowl, discarding solids. Transfer strained liquid to a pitcher or bowl.

4. Add remaining 2 cups (500 mL) of water, sugar and vanilla. Blend until sugar is dissolved. Serve immediately over ice and garnish with a cinnamon stick.

Mexican Hot Chocolate

Makes 4 servings

This warm beverage is a sweet blend of chocolate, cinnamon and vanilla. It is smooth, rich and delicious.

4 cups	milk	1 L
6 oz	semisweet chocolate, chopped	175 g
¼ cup	granulated sugar	60 mL
1 tsp	ground cinnamon	5 mL
1 tsp	vanilla extract	5 mL
1 tsp	almond extract	5 mL

1. In a medium saucepan, heat milk over medium-low heat. In a small bowl, combine chocolate, sugar and cinnamon and add to milk. Stir until well blended and heated through, 4 to 6 minutes. Add vanilla and almond extracts. Serve warm.

Café con Leche

Makes 4 servings

This creamy coffee is actually a Spanish beverage enjoyed by many around the world. It is a simple composition of coffee and milk.

2 cups	whole milk	500 mL
2 cups	strong black coffee, heated to high temperature	500 mL

1. In a small saucepan, heat milk over low heat until almost boiling. Place ½ cup (125 mL) of milk in each cup. Top each mug with ½ cup (125 mL) of coffee, stirring until well blended.

Café Dulce

Makes 1 serving

Dulce means sweet in Spanish. This is a popular coffee drink enjoyed throughout the day and is perfect for an after-dinner drink.

6 oz	strong black hot coffee	175 g
1 tbsp	caramel sauce	15 mL
2 tbsp	coffee-flavored liqueur, such as Kahlúa	30 mL
1 tsp	half-and-half (10%) cream	5 mL

1. Fill a mug with hot coffee. Add caramel sauce, liqueur and cream. Blend well and serve.

Variation

For a sweeter dessert-style drink, reduce Kahlúa by 1 tbsp (15 mL) and increase caramel sauce by 1 tbsp (15 mL).

Mexican Eggnog

**Makes 3 cups
(750 mL)**

Cinnamon and vanilla-
flavored eggnog is often
drizzled over desserts
in Mexico. *Rompope,* as
it is called, is a Mexican
specialty and enjoyed
as an after-dinner drink
as well. This recipe is
rich in flavor and simple
to make.

||||||||||||||||||||||||||||||||||||||||

Tip

I like to serve eggnog over
cracked ice with a splash of
rum on top.

● Double boiler

4 cups	milk	1 L
1 cup	granulated sugar	250 mL
1	piece (about 3-inches/7.5 cm) cinnamon stick	1
6	egg yolks	6
⅓ cup	rum	75 mL
1 tsp	vanilla extract	5 mL

1 In a large pot, bring milk, sugar and cinnamon stick
to a boil over medium-high heat. Do not stir. Using a
spoon, skim off and discard any skin that forms on the
top of the milk. Reduce heat to medium and let milk
boil until it reduces to about 3 cups (750 mL), 25 to
30 minutes.

2. Add 1-inch (2.5 cm) of water to a saucepan or double
boiler and simmer over medium heat. In double
boiler bowl or stainless-steel bowl, whisk egg yolks.
Place bowl over simmering water and slowly add milk
mixture, stirring constantly, until mixture thickens,
5 to 7 minutes.

3. Remove bowl from saucepan and place bowl in a
larger bowl with ice water. Whisk in rum and vanilla.
Mix well. Cover and let cool completely. Place in
an airtight container and refrigerate for 2 hours or
overnight before serving. Serve cold.

184   Beverages and Cocktails

Fresh Fruit Water

Makes 4 to 6 servings

Agua fresca are light refreshing fruit beverages found at the open markets and taco stands throughout Mexico. They are a nice complement to the rich chiles, herbs and spices of Mexican cuisine.

Watermelon Agua Fresca

● Blender

1	seedless watermelon (6 to 7 lbs/ 3 to 3.5 kg)	1
3 cups	cold water	750 mL
	Juice of 3 limes	
¼ cup	liquid honey	60 mL
	Ice	

1. Remove rind from watermelon and cut into chunks. In a blender, combine one-third of the watermelon with one-third of the water and blend until smooth. Strain watermelon mixture through a sieve into a pitcher or glass jar. Discard solids. Repeat with remaining watermelon and water.

2. Add lime juice and honey. Place in the refrigerator and chill for up to 3 hours. Serve over ice.

Strawberry Agua Fresca

● Blender

5 cups	fresh strawberries, hulled and sliced	1.25 L
4 cups	cold water	1 L
	Juice of 3 limes	
3 tbsp	liquid honey	45 mL
	Ice	
	Whole fresh strawberries	

1. In a blender, combine half of the strawberries and half of the water. Strain strawberry mixture through a sieve into a pitcher or glass jar. Discard solids. Repeat with remaining strawberries and water.

2. Stir in lime juice and honey. Place in the refrigerator and chill for up to 3 hours. Serve over ice. Garnish with whole berries.

Variation

For a sweeter beverage, add more honey to taste.

Margarita Martini

Makes 1 serving

This is a slow-sipping cocktail, which, according to many, is the true margarita. Fresh citrus crowns this martini perfectly.

Tip

There are a variety of orange liqueurs on the market such as Triple Sec, Cointreau or Grand Marnier. Experiment and find a favorite. I prefer the French liqueur, Cointreau.

- Shaker
- Martini glass

	Cracked ice	
1 oz	tequila	30 mL
1½ oz	orange-flavored liqueur (see Tip, left)	45 mL
2 tbsp	freshly squeezed lime juice	30 mL
1	orange peel twist (see Tip, below)	1

1. Fill a shaker half full with cracked ice. Pour in tequila, liqueur and lime juice. Shake well and strain into martini glass and garnish with an orange twist.

> ## Tip
>
> *To make an orange peel twist:* Using a slice of orange, remove the center and as much of the white pith as possible, leaving the orange strip of peel. Wrap the peel around a straw. Let set for 6 to 8 minutes. Remove from straw. It will have a loose curly shape.

Mini Margarita Shots

Makes 1 serving

Tequila lovers enjoy a straight shot of their favorite liquor. For those that want a smoother taste of tequila, try my brother, Mike's, favorite party starter.

Tips

When drinking toss it back quickly.

I like a smooth margarita mix that has a nice sweet-tart balance like Jose Cuervo.

- 2-oz (60 mL) shot glasses

1 oz	aged tequila	30 mL
1 oz	margarita mix (see Tips, left)	30 mL
1	lime wedge	1

1. Pour tequila into shot glass and top with margarita mix.
2. Top with a splash of lime.

Margarita Classico

IIIIIIIIIIIIIIIIIIIIIIIIIIIIIIIIIIIIIIIIIIIIIIIIIIIIIIIIIIIIIIIIIIIIIIIIIIIIIIIIIIIIIIIIIIIIIIIIIII

Makes 4 servings

This fresh and frosty cocktail is perfectly balanced — not too tart and not too sweet. The combination of tequila and beer gives it a kick with some flavor. Add some freshness by blending in luscious fruit and drizzling in sweet liqueurs to create the ultimate frozen margaritas (see Variations, right).

IIIIIIIIIIIIIIIIIIIIIIIIIIIIIIIIIIIIIIIIIII

Tip

For a thicker frozen margarita, reduce light beer to 1/2 cup (125 mL) and add more ice for desired consistency.

- Margarita glasses
- Blender

1	lime, cut into 5 wedges	1
	Kosher salt	
3/4 cup	frozen limeade concentrate	175 mL
3/4 cup	silver tequila	175 mL
1 1/2 oz	orange-flavored liqueur, such as Triple Sec, Cointreau or Grand Marnier	45 mL
3/4 cup	light beer	175 mL
5 cups	cracked ice, divided	1.25 L

1. Rub rim of each glass with a lime wedge. Dust with salt. Shake off any excess salt.

2. In blender, combine limeade, tequila, liqueur, beer and 3 cups (750 mL) of the ice and blend until slushy, 2 to 3 minutes. Add more ice, if desired. Pour into each glass and garnish each with a lime wedge.

Variations

Green Apple Margarita: Drizzle 1/2 oz (15 mL) green apple liqueur over each frozen margarita and garnish with a thin slice of Granny Smith apple.

Peach Margarita: Add 2 oz (60 mL) peach schnapps to the margarita mixture and blend. Garnish with fresh chopped peaches.

Mango Margarita: Add 1/2 cup (125 mL) fresh mango chunks to margarita mixture and blend. Garnish with fresh mango slices.

Strawberry Margarita: Reduce beer to 1/4 cup (60 mL). Follow Step 2, adding 1 cup (250 mL) puréed strawberries (about 15 strawberries). Blend well.

Pomegranate Margarita

Makes 1 serving

Fresh pomegranate juice layered with citrusy orange and lime creates the perfect balance in this special margarita.

● Shaker

2	lime wedges	2
	Superfine sugar	
	Cracked ice	
1 oz	silver tequila	30 mL
½ oz	orange-flavored liqueur, such as Triple Sec, Cointreau or Grand Marnier	15 mL
¼ cup	unsweetened pomegranate juice	60 mL
	Club soda	

1. Rub rim of glass with a lime wedge. Dust with sugar. Shake off any excess sugar.

2. Fill a shaker half full of ice. Add tequila, liqueur and pomegranate juice. Shake for 30 to 45 seconds. Strain into glass. Top with club soda and garnish with remaining lime wedge.

Variation

For sweet savory flavor, substitute kosher salt for the sugared rim.

Chile Rita

This is my rendition of a special margarita originally created by my friends at La Posta, a historic Mexican Restaurant in New Mexico. The combination of a sweet, fruity syrup with a bite of chile and tequila is unforgettable.

Tips

Transfer remaining jam mixture to a sealed jar and refrigerate for up to 2 weeks.

Use a high-quality prepared liquid margarita mix with a medium sweet-sour balance.

● Margarita glass

¾ cup	boysenberry or raspberry jam	175 mL
1 tsp	hot pepper flakes	5 mL
2	lime wedges	2
	Kosher salt	
	Cracked ice	
1 oz	silver tequila	30 mL
½ cup	liquid margarita mix (see Tips, left)	125 mL

1. In a small pot, combine jam and hot pepper flakes and heat over medium-low heat, stirring, until jam is melted. Strain through a colander or strainer into a bowl to remove seeds and flakes. Let cool to room temperature.

2. Rub rim of glass with lime and dust with salt. Shake off any excess salt. Fill shaker half full of ice. Add tequila and 1 tbsp (15 mL) of jam mixture. Top with margarita mix and shake for 1 minute. Pour into glass and garnish with remaining lime wedge.

Pink Cadillac Margarita Punch

Makes 12 servings

This margarita is a party favorite. Serving it "punch style" makes it easy on the host. The sweet grenadine takes the tartness away, creating a smooth cocktail you can enjoy all evening.

- 1 punch bowl
- Highball glasses

1	bottle (1.75 L) margarita mix (see Tips, page 189)	1
1½ cups	gold tequila	375 mL
⅓ cup	grenadine	75 mL
4 to 5	limes, divided	4 to 5
	Cracked ice	
	Kosher salt	

1. In a punch or serving bowl, combine margarita mix, tequila and grenadine. Cut 2 of the limes into thin slices and add to mixture. Add lots of cracked ice.

2. Cut the remaining limes into wedges. Rub rim of each glass with a lime wedge and dust with salt. Shake off any excess salt. Fill each glass with ice. Top with punch and garnish with remaining lime wedges.

> ### Variation
> Substitute ½ cup (125 mL) cranberry cocktail or pomegranate juice for the grenadine.

Mock-Margarita Cocktail

Makes 4 servings

I love this simple, light non-alcoholic punch. My friend Janet and I created this for an afternoon gathering and it was a hit! It is a citrusy, bubbly delight.

- 4 stemmed glasses

6 oz	frozen limeade concentrate	175 g
l quart	tonic water	1 L
	Ice	
2	limes, cut in thin slices	2
	Mint leaves	

1. In a large pitcher, combine concentrate and tonic water. Blend well. Fill each glass with ice and garnish with one lime slice and one mint leaf.

White Wine Margarita

Makes 4 servings

This is a luscious frozen cocktail for wine lovers. It is a perfect margarita with a lighter alcohol content and flavor. The citrus juices and wine blend well in this frosty drink.

Tip

A rich full-bodied Chardonnay works well with the recipe, or try a Sauvignon Blanc for a crisp lighter flavor.

- Blender
- Margarita glasses

½ cup	Chardonnay (see Tip, left)	125 mL
6 oz	frozen limeade concentrate	175 mL
½ cup	freshly squeezed orange juice	125 mL
3 cups	cracked ice	750 mL
2	limes, cut into thin wedges	2
	Kosher salt	
1	orange, sliced into quarters	1

1. In a blender, combine wine, limeade and orange juice and blend for 1 minute. Slowly add ice and blend to a slushy consistency.

2. Rub rims of each glass with lime wedge and dust with salt. Shake off any excess salt. Fill each glass with margarita mixture. Garnish with a twisted orange slice.

Michilada

Makes 1 serving

Pronounced *Mee-chil-ada*, this cool cocktail takes the beer with a twist of lime to the next level. Adding fresh citrus juices to your favorite beer creates a light and refreshing cocktail.

Tip

There are a variety of Mexican beers on the market, such as Corona, Pacifico, Tecate and Dos Equis just to name a few. They all vary in taste, so try them and find your favorites.

- Collins glass

	Cracked ice	
¼ cup	freshly squeezed lime or orange juice	60 mL
1	bottle (12 oz/341 mL) Mexican beer (see Tip, left)	1
1 to 2	lime or orange slices	1 to 2

1. Fill glass half full with cracked ice. Add lime juice. Top with beer. Garnish with floating lime slices and serve. Add remaining beer to the glass as needed.

Chavela

Makes 1 serving

This is a spicy beer cocktail that combines a tomato base with a Mexican beer.

- Collins glass

	Cracked ice	
¼ cup	tomato juice	60 mL
½ tsp	hot pepper sauce	2 mL
1 tsp	Worcestershire sauce	5 mL
1	bottle (12 oz/341 mL) Mexican beer (see Tip, above)	1
1 to 2	lemon wedges	1 to 2

1. Fill glass half full with cracked ice. Add tomato juice. Add hot pepper sauce and Worcestershire sauce. Top with beer. Garnish with lemon wedge and serve. Add remaining beer to the glass as needed.

Tequila Shots

Makes 1 serving

Shooting tequila is a ritual we cherish in the West but it's not for the faint of heart or the averse to alcohol. A little salt, a shot of tequila and a little lime all add to the mystery. Tequila should not choke you or taste bad. There are some fine tequilas that are just right for sipping or shooting. Select a smooth-tasting tequila. Here is the popular and historical methodology.

	Salt	
1 to 2 oz	fine tequila	30 to 60 mL
	Lime wedge	

1. Line up salt, tequila shot and lime wedge. Lick the area between your forefinger and thumb.

2. Pour salt on the wet spot. Yell, "Uno, dos, tres!" Lick salt and quickly drink (or shoot) the tequila. Grab your lime wedge and bite into it, squeezing as much juice into your mouth as possible. Salud!

Cactus Colada

Makes 4 servings

This Hawaiian cocktail gets a zing from a shot of tequila and a twist of lime, creating a Southwest surprise.

- Preheat oven to 350°F (180°C)
- Blender
- Collins glass

½ cup	sweetened flaked coconut	125 mL
1 cup	unsweetened pineapple juice	250 mL
½ cup	gold tequila	125 mL
½ cup	cream of coconut	125 mL
	Juice of 2 limes	
3 to 4 cups	cracked ice	750 mL to 1 L

1. Place coconut flakes on a baking sheet and bake in preheated oven until lightly browned, 6 to 8 minutes. Let cool completely.

2. In a blender, combine pineapple juice, tequila, cream of coconut, lime juice and 3 cups (750 mL) of ice and blend until ice is smooth, 2 to 3 minutes. Add more ice for a thicker consistency. Pour into serving glasses. Garnish each cocktail with toasted coconut.

Sangrita

Makes 4 servings

Sangrita (not to be confused with Sangria, the fruity wine beverage) means "little blood" in Spanish. This little sipper was created as a tequila chaser and has become a Mexican tradition. It is a careful combination of flavors that enhance the taste of premium tequilas.

Tip

I like Louisiana Hot Sauce, however, Tabasco is delicious as well.

- 2-oz (60 mL) shot glasses

1 cup	tomato juice	250 mL
¼ cup	freshly squeezed orange juice	60 mL
¼ cup	freshly squeezed lime juice	60 mL
1 tbsp	grenadine	15 mL
2 tsp	hot pepper sauce (see Tip, left)	10 mL
1 tsp	Worcestershire sauce	5 mL
	Tequila	

1. In a small pitcher, combine tomato juice, orange juice, lime juice, grenadine, hot pepper sauce and Worcestershire sauce. Mix well. Take a shot of tequila and sip the Sangrita.

Variation

Combine the tequila and the Sangrita together and sip. This is known as a *Completo* in the Mexican culture.

Mexican Mojito

Makes 1 serving

The mojito cocktail, Cuba's oldest cocktail usually made with rum, is tantalizing with tequila. Muddling the fresh mint and lime adds an intense flavor to this cocktail.

- Muddling stick
- Tall glass

8	mint leaves, divided	8
1 tbsp	granulated sugar	15 mL
1	lime, sliced into quarters	1
2 oz	silver tequila	60 mL
	Cracked ice	
	Club soda	

1. In a glass, add 7 mint leaves, sugar and lime. Muddle until sugar is almost dissolved and flavors are blended. Add tequila and fill with ice. Top with club soda and stir. Garnish with remaining mint leaf.

Mexican Madras Martini

Makes 1 serving

This martini is full of flavor. Orange, cranberry and fresh lime create a luscious martini.

- Shaker
- Martini glass

	Cracked ice	
1 oz	tequila	30 mL
1 oz	orange juice	30 mL
1 oz	cranberry juice	30 mL
	Splash of freshly squeezed lime juice	

1. Fill a shaker half full of cracked ice. Pour in tequila, orange juice and cranberry juice. Shake well and strain into a martini glass and add a splash of lime juice.

Dulce de Leche Martini

Makes 1 serving

This is a seductively sweet caramel cocktail inspired by the dulce de leche (*Dool-say deh Lechay*) candies you will find in Mexico. It makes a wonderful after-dinner drink, especially after Mexican fare!

Tip

Test the different caramel sauces on the market. I like one flavored with a hint of salt.

- Shaker
- Martini glass

	Cracked ice	
½ oz	rum	15 mL
2 tbsp	heavy or whipping (35%) cream	30 mL
2 tbsp	caramel sauce (see Tip, left)	30 mL

1. Fill a shaker half full of cracked ice. Pour in rum. Add cream and caramel sauce. Shake well and strain into a unique martini glass.

Tequila Sunrise

Makes 1 serving

I love serving these for brunch or an early tailgate party on game day. They are smooth and go well with my breakfast tacos. The pomegranate syrup is a sweet natural alternative to the traditional splash of grenadine.

● Collins or highball glass

	Cracked ice	
1½ oz	gold tequila	45 mL
6 tbsp	freshly squeezed orange juice	90 mL
1 tbsp	grenadine	15 mL
1	lime wedge	1

1. Fill glass with cracked ice. Top with tequila and orange juice. Slowly add grenadine. Let settle on bottom of glass. Serve with lime wedge.

Variation

If you want a slightly different taste, replace grenadine with 1 tbsp (15 mL) Pomegranate Simple Syrup (below).

Pomegranate Simple Syrup

Makes 1½ cups (375 mL)

2 cups	unsweetened pomegranate juice	500 mL
¼ cup	superfine sugar	60 mL
1 tbsp	freshly squeezed lemon juice	15 mL

1. In a small pot, combine pomegranate juice and sugar and bring to a boil over medium heat, stirring, until sugar is dissolved. Add lemon juice. Reduce heat and boil gently until reduced by about one-third and syrupy. Let cool to room temperature. Transfer to an airtight container and refrigerate for up to 5 days.

Bloody Mary Bar

Makes 12 servings	

I have tasted many Bloody Marys and I have loved them all. With so many different ingredients, the options are endless. Create a special little area at your party where guests can go wild and make the perfect Bloody Mary, whatever the flavors may be!

- Blender
- 1 pitcher
- Collins glasses

2 cups	Tomato Table Salsa (page 57) or store-bought	500 mL
1	can (48 oz/1.36 L) tomato juice	1
	Cracked ice	
1¼ cups	vodka	300 mL
2 tbsp	Worcestershire sauce	30 mL
1 tbsp	prepared horseradish	15 mL

1. In a blender, purée salsa until smooth.

2. In a pitcher, combine salsa purée and tomato juice and refrigerate until chilled, for at least 30 minutes or up to 4 hours.

3. Fill a Collins glass half full with cracked ice. Pour in 1 oz (30 mL) of vodka. Top with tomato mixture. Add ½ tsp (2 mL) of the Worcestershire sauce and ¼ tsp (1 mL) of the horseradish into each Bloody Mary. Add garnish as desired (see Bloody Mary Bar, below).

Variation

Bloody Maria: Substitute a premium tequila for the vodka.

Bloody Mary Bar

Set out small bowls of any of the following for garnish: whole pickled garlic cloves, hot pepper flakes, cracked black peppercorns, kosher salt, ground cumin, garlic powder, celery sticks, baby dill pickles, yellow chile peppers, jalapeños, snow peas, sugar snap peas, chunks of cucumber, chopped green onions, Greek olives, chopped roasted New Mexico or Anaheim green chile (page 98), pickled okra, minced cilantro and a variety of hot sauces, such as Fiesta Taco Sauce (page 66), Salsa Verde (page 58), Green Chile and Jalapeño Salsa (page 58).

Sangria

Makes 12 servings

Sangria is a traditional wine-based punch made with red wine and seasonal fruit. This cocktail will add a festive feeling to any gathering.

● 1 pitcher

1	bottle (750 mL) dry red wine, such as Cabernet Sauvignon, Shiraz, Merlot or Zinfandel	1
1 tbsp	granulated sugar	15 mL
	Juice of 1 orange	
	Juice of 1 lemon	
1	orange, thinly sliced	1
1	lemon, thinly sliced	1
2	peaches, diced	2
1 cup	sparkling water	250 mL
	Ice	

1. In a large pitcher, combine wine, sugar, orange juice and lemon juice. Add orange slices, lemon slices and diced peach. Refrigerate overnight to ensure flavors infuse. Just before serving, stir in sparkling water. Serve in tall glasses half full of ice.

White Summer Sangria

Makes 18 to 24 servings

This is the perfect fruity spritzer for a hot afternoon or a mid-morning brunch. Serve it in a large glass pitcher or punch bowl.

Tip

Sauvignon Blanc is a good selection for this sangria.

⅓ cup	brandy	75 mL
⅓ cup	peach schnapps	75 mL
2	bottles (each 750 mL) dry white wine (see Tip, left)	2
1 tbsp	granulated sugar	15 mL
1	orange, thinly sliced	1
1	lemon, thinly sliced	1
1	peach, peeled and diced	1
1	bottle (12 oz/375 mL) sparkling water	1

1. In a large pitcher, combine brandy, schnapps, wine and sugar, stirring until sugar is dissolved. Add orange slices, lemon slices and diced peach and refrigerate overnight. Serve in wine goblets with fruit in each one and top each with sparkling water.

Desserts

Spicy Fruit and Crème

Makes 6 servings		

Years ago in Mexico I enjoyed this fresh fruit plate at a patio café. Fresh fruit and jicama sprinkled with a hint of chile and citrus was an addictive combination. It is delightful after a Mexican dinner.

3 cups	chopped pineapple (bite-size pieces)	750 mL
1 cup	chopped peeled jicama	250 mL
3	kiwi, peeled and cut into bite-size pieces	3
	Juice of 2 limes	
	Grated zest and juice of 1 orange	
½ cup	sour cream	125 mL
½ cup	vanilla-flavored Greek yogurt	125 mL
1 cup	raspberries	250 mL
2 tsp	hot pepper flakes	10 mL

1. In a large bowl, gently toss together pineapple, jicama, kiwi, lime juice, orange zest, and orange juice. Cover and refrigerate until chilled, stirring occasionally, for 30 minutes or for up to 2 hours.

2. In a medium bowl, combine sour cream and yogurt and mix well.

3. Before serving, arrange fruit on a platter. Top with raspberries and sprinkle with pepper flakes. Serve with sour cream mixture for dipping.

Caramel Flan

Makes 6 servings

This rich custard is a delightful dessert after a spicy Mexican meal. Flan is a traditional favorite that can be enjoyed with the simple caramel flavor or garnished with coconut and fresh fruits.

Variations

Garnish flans with ¾ cup (175 mL) sweetened shredded coconut, ½ cup (125 mL) raspberries or ¼ cup (60 mL) slivered almonds just before serving.

- Preheat oven to 350°F (180°C)
- Six 6-oz (175 g) ramekins, greased
- 13- by 9-inch (33 by 23 cm) glass baking dish

¾ cup	granulated sugar, divided	175 mL
2 tbsp	water	30 mL
3	eggs	3
1 cup	milk	250 mL
1	can (14 oz or 300 mL) sweetened condensed milk	1
½ tsp	vanilla extract	2 mL
Pinch	salt	Pinch

1. In a small saucepan over medium-low heat, combine ½ cup (125 mL) of the sugar and water. Bring to a boil, stirring constantly, until sugar is dissolved. Boil, stirring, until syrup is caramel-colored, 10 to 12 minutes. Carefully and quickly pour syrup into ramekins, swirling caramel around bottom and sides of each ramekin. Set aside.

2. In a large bowl, whisk eggs until well beaten. Using a wooden spoon, stir in ¼ cup (60 mL) of remaining sugar, milk, sweetened condensed milk, vanilla and salt. Mix well being careful not to over whip the egg mixture since this will create air pockets when baking.

3. Pour egg mixture into ramekins, dividing equally. Carefully place each ramekin in baking dish. Fill dish with 1-inch (2.5 cm) of hot water. Bake in preheated oven until center of each custard is firm and a knife inserted in the center comes out clean, 25 to 35 minutes. Remove ramekins from baking dish and let cool on a rack for 1 hour.

4. Cover and refrigerate until chilled for at least 1 hour or for up to 4 hours. To serve, run a knife around the edge to loosen the custard. Invert each ramekin on individual plates and turn flans. Remove ramekins, allowing the caramel topping to cover the top of the flan.

Sopapillas de Fruit

Heavenly sopapillas filled with luscious berries laced with citrus are delectable. This warm pastry can be served for dessert or for brunch.

Tip

This recipe calls for eight 5-inch (12.5 cm) sopapillas, which is half of the recipe on page 81. However, you can use store-bought sopapilla mix as well.

½	recipe Sopapillas (page 81), slightly cooled (see Tip, left)	½
1 cup	raspberries	250 mL
1 cup	diced strawberries	250 mL
¾ cup	blueberries	175 mL
1 tbsp	granulated sugar	15 mL
2 tbsp	orange-flavored liqueur, such as Triple Sec, Cointreau or Grand Marnier	30 mL
	Grated zest of 1 lime	
2 tbsp	confectioner's (icing) sugar	30 mL

1. In a large bowl, toss together raspberries, strawberries, blueberries, sugar, liqueur and lime zest. Cover and refrigerate until chilled, stirring occasionally, for 1 hour or for up to 3 hours.

2. Before serving, slice one edge of each sopapilla and place on individual plates. Divide berry mixture equally and spoon inside of each sopapilla. Dust with confectioner's sugar and serve.

Bizcochitos

Makes 36 cookies

In 1989, the bizcochito became the official cookie for the state of New Mexico. This traditional holiday cookie is a combination of anise and cinnamon with a hint of brandy.

Tips

I like using a star- or flower-shaped cookie cutter. However, if you are pressed for time, roll dough into 1-inch (2.5 cm) balls, place on baking sheets and press to ¼-inch (0.5 cm) thickness. Bake as directed.

Store in an airtight container at room temperature for up to 2 days or freeze for up to 2 months.

- Preheat oven to 350°F (180°C)
- 1-inch (2.5 cm) cookie cutters, any shape
- Baking sheets, greased

3 cups	all-purpose flour	750 mL
1½ tsp	baking powder	7 mL
Pinch	salt	Pinch
1 cup	lard	250 mL
1½ cups	granulated sugar, divided	375 mL
1 tsp	anise seeds	5 mL
1	egg	1
2 tbsp	brandy	30 mL
1 tbsp	ground cinnamon	15 mL

1. In a large bowl, sift together flour, baking powder and salt. In a separate bowl, using an electric mixer on medium speed, cream together lard, ¾ cup (175 mL) of the sugar and anise until fluffy. Continue mixing and add egg. Beat until well blended, about 2 minutes, scraping the sides.

2. Reduce speed on mixer to low and beat in flour mixture and brandy until well blended. Cover and refrigerate until chilled, for at least 1 hour or for up to 3 hours.

3. In a small bowl, combine remaining ¾ cup (175 mL) of sugar and cinnamon. Set aside.

4. On a lightly floured surface, roll dough out to ¼-inch (0.5 cm) thickness. Using 1-inch (2.5 cm) cookie cutters, cut into desired shapes, re-rolling scraps. Place on prepared baking sheet, 2 inches (5 cm) apart. Bake in preheated oven until firm and slightly browned, 10 to 12 minutes. Let cool on baking sheets for 2 to 4 minutes. Dip while warm into cinnamon mixture and place on wire rack to cool completely.

Variations

For a buttery flavor, substitute 1 cup (250 mL) softened butter for the lard.

You may also substitute sweet red wine for brandy.

Mexican Wedding Cookies

Makes 36 cookies

This cookie is similar to a shortbread cookie with a nutty depth of flavor. Mexican wedding cookies, also known as *polvorones* (which means powder), are baked then generously dipped in confectioner's sugar for sweetness.

Tip

Store in an airtight container at room temperature for up to 2 days or freeze for up to 2 months.

- Preheat oven to 400°F (200°C)
- Baking sheets, greased

1 cup	butter, softened	250 mL
1½ cups	confectioner's (icing) sugar, divided	375 mL
⅔ cup	very finely chopped pecans	150 mL
1 tsp	vanilla extract	5 mL
2¼ cups	all-purpose flour	550 mL
¼ tsp	salt	1 mL

1. In a large bowl, using an electric mixer on medium speed, cream together butter, ½ cup (125 mL) of the sugar, pecans and vanilla until fluffy, about 2 minutes. Gradually mix in flour and salt until until well blended and dough holds together, scraping the sides, about 2 minutes.

2. Shape into 1-inch (2.5 cm) balls. Place on prepared baking sheet, 2 inches (5 cm) apart. Press each cookie to flatten slightly to about ½-inch (1 cm) thickness.

3. Place remaining confectioner's sugar on a plate.

4. Bake cookies in preheated oven until slightly browned and edges are firm, 12 to 14 minutes. Roll warm cookies immediately in remaining confectioner's sugar. Place cookies on a wire rack and let cool completely.

Mexican Sweet Churros

Makes about sixteen 4–inch (10 cm) churros	

Everyone loves churros! They are a simple dough that is fried and sugared. These sweet, warm pastries will melt in your mouth.

Tips

The dough can be prepared up to 3 hours ahead. Cover and keep at room temperature, then continue with Steps 3 and 4.

Check for doneness in the center. Churros should be soft in the center but not doughy.

- Cookie press with a ⅜-inch (9 mm) tip or pastry bag and ⅜-inch (9 mm) star tip
- Baking sheet, greased
- Candy/deep-fry thermometer

1 cup + 2 tbsp	granulated sugar , divided	280 mL
2 tsp	ground cinnamon	10 mL
1 tsp	kosher salt, divided	5 mL
1 cup	water	250 mL
2 tbsp	shortening	30 mL
1 cup	all-purpose flour	250 mL
	Oil	

1. In a pie plate, combine 1 cup (250 mL) of the sugar, cinnamon and ½ tsp (2 mL) of the kosher salt. Set aside.

2. In a medium saucepan, combine water, shortening, 2 tbsp (30 mL) of the sugar and ½ tsp (2 mL) of salt. Bring to a boil over high heat. Boil, stirring, for 1 minute. Remove from heat and add flour, stirring until mixture forms a soft dough ball. Transfer dough to a bowl and let cool.

3. Place dough into cookie press and press out 4-inch (10 cm) long churros onto prepared baking sheet.

4. Fill a deep fryer, deep heavy pot or deep skillet with 3 inches (7.5 cm) of oil and heat to 350°F (180°C). Using tongs, gently place 3 to 4 churros at a time into the hot oil and deep-fry, turning once, until golden brown and crispy on the ends and a bit soft in the middle, 2 to 3 minutes. Using a slotted spoon, transfer to a baking sheet lined with paper towels to drain. Roll warm churros in cinnamon mixture until they are well coated. Serve warm.

Variation

For a nutty flavor, add 2 tbsp (30 mL) finely ground pecans to the dough in Step 2.

Mexican Chocolate Brownie

Makes 6 to
8 servings

This thin, rich brownie has a hint of cinnamon that adds a different element of flavor. The fudgy icing is decadent and delicious.

Tips

Select a basic brownie mix, not a chewy-style mix. Choose one that requires twice as much water than oil. I also add an extra egg for a fluffier brownie than what is called for in the basic instructions.

Brownies can be made ahead. Let cool completely. Store in an airtight container at room temperature for up to 2 days or freeze for up to 3 months.

- Preheat oven to 350°F (180°C)
- 13- by 9-inch (33 by 23 cm) glass baking dish, greased

1	package (19 oz/540 g) basic brownie mix (see Tips, left)	1
2 tsp	ground cinnamon	10 mL
½ cup	water	125 mL
¼ cup	oil	60 mL
3	eggs, beaten	3

Icing

½ cup	butter	125 mL
2 tbsp	unsweetened cocoa powder	30 mL
3 tbsp	milk	45 mL
1 tsp	vanilla extract	5 mL
2½ cups	confectioner's (icing) sugar	625 mL
1½ tsp	ground cinnamon	7 mL

1. In a large bowl, combine brownie mix and cinnamon. Using an electric mixer on low speed, add water, oil and eggs, beating until well blended, 2 to 3 minutes. Pour into prepared baking dish and bake in preheated oven until knife comes out clean when inserted in center, 20 to 25 minutes. Let cool completely in dish on a wire rack.

2. *Icing:* In a medium saucepan, melt butter over medium-low heat. Stir in cocoa until well blended. Continue stirring and add milk and vanilla. Remove from heat. Gradually add confectioner's sugar and cinnamon, mixing until smooth and well blended. Pour over cooled brownies and let icing set at room temperature for 30 to 45 minutes.

Variations

For a nutty icing, add 1 cup (250 mL) coarsely chopped pecans to the icing after the sugar and cinnamon.

For a thicker brownie, use an 11- by 7-inch (28 by 18 cm) baking dish. Increase baking time to 25 to 30 minutes.

Spiced Pecans

Makes 4 cups (1 L)		

Sweet and spicy pecans are a delicious treat to offer your guests with cocktails or during dessert. These tasty little nuts are also delicious over ice cream and flan.

- Preheat oven to 225°F (110°C)
- Rimmed baking sheet, greased

1	egg white	1
1 tsp	cold water	5 mL
4 cups	pecan pieces	1 L
1 cup	granulated sugar	250 mL
1 tsp	ground cinnamon	5 mL
1 tsp	cayenne pepper	5 mL
½ tsp	salt	2 mL

1. In a medium bowl, using an electric mixer on medium speed, beat egg white and water until frothy, about 2 minutes. Using a wooden spoon, stir in pecan pieces until well coated.

2. In a small bowl, combine sugar, cinnamon, cayenne pepper and salt. Pour over pecans and mix until well coated.

3. Spread pecans on prepared baking sheet. Bake in preheated oven, stirring occasionally, until sugar coating is firm and dry, 20 to 25 minutes. Let pecans cool completely. Store in an airtight container for up to 1 week.

Mexican Sundae

Makes 4 servings

This fun Mexican sundae is easy to make and leaves an impression on your guests. Smooth creamy chocolate fudge is delicious with sweet and savory pecans.

Tip

Store extra sauce in an airtight container and refrigerate for up to 2 weeks. To reheat, place sauce in a microwave-safe bowl and microwave on Medium for 1-minute intervals until heated through.

1	can (14 oz or 300 mL) sweetened condensed milk	1
2 tbsp	butter	30 mL
¾ cup	semisweet chocolate chips	175 mL
1 tsp	vanilla extract	5 mL
4	large scoops vanilla ice cream	4
1 cup	Spiced Pecans (page 207)	250 mL

1. In a medium saucepan, combine sweetened condensed milk, butter and chocolate chips. Heat, stirring often, until chips are melted, 6 to 8 minutes. Remove from heat and add vanilla. Mix well.

2. Place each scoop of ice cream in individual bowls. Drizzle desired amount of chocolate sauce over each scoop. Divide pecans evenly among each sundae. Serve immediately.

Variation

Add 1 tsp (5 mL) ground cinnamon in Step 1.

Margarita Pie

Makes 6 servings

Refreshing, simple flavors of a margarita infused into a dessert are exceptional. This margarita pie is light and luscious and quick to make!

Tip

Use a high-quality prepared liquid margarita mix with a medium sweet-sour balance.

● Preheat oven to 350°F (180°C)

2	eggs	2
2	egg yolks	2
1/4 cup	freshly squeezed lime juice	60 mL
1	can (14 oz or 300 mL) sweetened condensed milk	1
1/3 cup	liquid margarita mix (see Tip, left)	75 mL
3	drops green food coloring	3
1	(9-inch/23 cm) store-bought vanilla-flavored cookie crumb crust	1
1 cup	heavy or whipping (35%) cream	250 mL
1/2 cup	granulated sugar	125 mL
1	lime, thinly sliced	1

1. In a medium bowl, using an electric mixer, beat eggs and egg yolks until thick and pale, about 2 minutes. Continue mixing and add lime juice, condensed milk, margarita mix and food coloring and beat for 2 to 3 minutes.

2. Pour into pie shell and bake in preheated oven until center is firm, about 25 minutes. Let cool completely. Cover and refrigerate until chilled for at least 1 hour or for up to 4 hours.

3. Just before serving, in a medium chilled bowl, using an electric mixer on medium-high speed, beat whipping cream and sugar until soft peaks form, 6 to 8 minutes. Serve slices of pie on individual plates topped with whipped cream and garnished with lime slices.

Variation

Substitute a 9-inch (23 cm) store-bought graham cracker-flavored crumb crust for the vanilla-flavored crumb crust.

Mexican Chocolate Pecan Pie

Makes 6 servings

This pecan pie has layers of flavor. I use a premade store-bought pie crust to save time and then whip up the filling in a matter of minutes. The chocolate, cinnamon and nut combination is decadent.

● Preheat oven to 400°F (200°C)

¼ cup	butter, softened	60 mL
½ cup	granulated sugar	125 mL
1 tsp	ground cinnamon	5 mL
3	eggs	3
1 cup	dark (golden) corn syrup	250 mL
4 oz	semisweet chocolate, coarsely chopped	125 g
1½ cups	pecans, coarsely chopped	375 mL
1	9-inch (23 cm) unbaked pie crust	1

1. In a large bowl, combine butter, sugar and cinnamon. Using an electric mixer on medium speed, beat in eggs and corn syrup. Using a rubber spatula, fold in chocolate pieces and pecans. Pour pecan mixture into unbaked pie crust.

2. Bake pie in preheated oven for 10 minutes. Reduce oven temperature to 300°F (150°C) and bake until crust is slightly browned and filling is firmly set, 35 to 40 minutes. Let cool completely on a wire rack.

Mexican Chocolate Cakes

Makes 6 servings	

This is a family favorite... rich mounds of chocolate with just a hint of cinnamon and chile. I love serving them warm with a scoop of vanilla ice cream.

- Preheat oven to 425°F (220°C)
- Six 4- to 6-oz (125 to 175 mL) ramekins, greased

4 oz	semisweet (dark) chocolate, coarsely chopped	125 g
½ cup	butter	125 mL
2	eggs	2
2	egg yolks	2
½ cup	granulated sugar	125 mL
1 tsp	ground cinnamon	5 mL
½ tsp	ancho chile powder	2 mL
⅓ cup	all-purpose flour	75 mL
	Vanilla or coffee ice cream	

1. In a small saucepan over low heat, melt chocolate and butter. Set aside.

2. In a medium bowl, using an electric mixer, beat eggs, egg yolks, sugar, cinnamon and chile until well blended, about 3 minutes. On low speed, gradually beat in the chocolate mixture until well blended. Increase speed to medium and beat until mixture is light and fluffy, about 3 minutes. Using a rubber spatula, stir in flour until blended.

3. Divide chocolate mixture equally among ramekins. Place ramekins on a baking sheet and bake in preheated oven until firm on top and cakes pull away from the sides of ramekins, 16 to 18 minutes. Run a knife around the edges of each ramekin. Invert on individual plates and serve hot with a scoop of vanilla or coffee ice cream.

Tres Leches Cake

Makes 6 to
8 servings

This sweet cake is a traditional cake soaked in a creamy milk mixture, made with three types of milk, and is loved by many. *Pastel de tres leches* (or three milk sweet cake), chilled and topped with cream, is served for many special occasions.

Variation

Garnish with ½ cup (125 mL) slivered almonds and/or flaked coconut.

- Preheat oven to 350°F (180°C)
- 13- by 9-inch (33 by 23 cm) glass baking dish, greased and lightly floured

1	can (14 oz or 300 mL) sweetened condensed milk	1
1	can (12 oz or 370 mL) evaporated milk	1
1 cup	whole milk	250 mL
2 tsp	vanilla extract	10 mL
1	package (18 oz/515 g) white cake mix	1
1 cup	water	250 mL
⅓ cup	oil	75 mL
3	eggs, slightly beaten	3
1 cup	heavy or whipping (35%) cream	250 mL
¾ cup	granulated sugar	175 mL

1. In a large saucepan, combine sweetened condensed milk, evaporated milk, whole milk and vanilla. Bring to a boil over medium heat, stirring constantly. Boil for 1 minute. Remove from heat. Cover and let cool completely.

2. In a large bowl, combine cake mix, water and oil. Using an electric mixer on medium speed, blend until smooth, 2 to 3 minutes. Continue mixing and add eggs, beating until well blended, 2 to 3 minutes. Pour into prepared baking pan. Bake in preheated oven until done in the center, 25 to 30 minutes.

3. Pierce cake with a long 2-pronged fork every 1 to 2 inches (2.5 to 5 cm). Pour milk mixture over cake, saturating every surface. Refrigerate for at least 2 hours or overnight.

4. Just before serving, in a medium chilled bowl, using an electric mixer on medium-high speed, beat whipping cream and sugar until peaks form, 6 to 8 minutes. Serve cake on individual plates and top with whipped cream.

Library and Archives Canada Cataloguing in Publication

Coffeen, Kelley
  200 easy Mexican recipes : authentic recipes from burritos to enchiladas /
Kelley Cleary Coffeen.

Includes index.
ISBN 978-0-7788-0436-9

  1. Cooking, Mexican. 2. Cookbooks. I. Title. II. Title: Two hundred
easy Mexican recipes.

TX716.M4C63 2013   641.5972   C2012-907494-2

Index

|||||||||||||||||||||||||||||||||||||||||||||||||||||||||||||||||||||||||||||||||||||||||||||||||||||||